Now What? What Now?

Sermons Matter

Mario Bolivar

Now What? What Now?
ISBN: Softcover 978-1-946478-09-2
Copyright © 2017 by Mario Bolivar

All rights reserved. No part of this book may be reproduced or transmitted in any form or by any means, electronic or mechanical, including photocopying, recording, or by any information storage and retrieval system, without permission in writing from the publisher.

To order additional copies of this book, contact:

Parson's Porch Books
1-423-310-8815
www.parsonsporch.com

Parson's Porch Books is an imprint of **Parson's Porch & Book Publishers** in Cleveland, Tennessee, which has double focus. We focus on the needs of creative writers who need a professional publisher to get their work to market, **&** we also focus on the needs of others by sharing our profits with those who struggle in poverty to meet their basic needs of food, clothing, shelter and safety.

Now What? What Now?

Table of Contents

Dedication	7
Now What? What Now?	9
Look Outside!	15
See and Repeat	20
The Good Shepherd	27
Happy Birthday, Church	32
Since You Called Me to Be with You!	36
Between a Rock and a Hard Place	41
Who's Your Father?	48
The Gift of Fear	53
Back to Basics: Confession of Belhar	58
Unity, Reconciliation, and Justice	64
Water. What is it Good for?	69
What Should We Do to Get Ready?	75
What Should We Do Once We Are Ready?	80
Are You a Procrastinator?	86
Serve One Another	89
The Illness of Vanity	93
Talk about Giving	98
Christ the King	102
Remembering Your Baptism	107
Mario Version 20.1.4	111

Dedication

To Troy Presbyterian Church, for taking the chance. To Skaneateles Presbyterian Church, for allowing me the privilege to be your Associate Pastor. To Mel, empowered by the Holy Spirit, my best sermons come often from something you said. Dante, for helping me understand the love of the Father. Omar David, for taking the first step. To mi vieja Gina y el Juancho, for the unconditional love. Ed and Richard, without you, I would have made the mistake of becoming a successful lawyer.

Soli Deo gloria.

Now What? What Now?

Recently I watched a movie called "The Martian" with Matt Damon. It is a history that will make you say "really... now what?" when something impossible happens. I am sure some of you are like me, and you love these kind of movies, but I know they are not for everyone. Today, I want you to consider what happens when those fascinating stories are not on the screen, rather when in fact they are your story or the story of someone that you know. Do not think about the NASA spaceships or actual fast cars or super and very real high jumps. Instead, consider those average times or events that belong in a movie, but that they are true stories or real events. Like the time you did not get in a car accident by an inch, or when you were stuck in a tight spot and a person-angel came out of nowhere and saved the day, and since then you became best friends.

Today I want to invite you to consider those times that make you say, "Now What?" --- but do not take it to the downside. We not only say "Now What?" when bad stuff happens, but we also say it when good stuff happens. Like the time on September 16th at 3:15 pm when my son was born, and I said, "Now What?" with a smile on my face. "Now What?" can denote a positive attitude rather than its nemesis, the infamous "What now?", characterized by a whining voice next to over extended, dragging feet and dropped shoulders.

The difference between "Now what?" and "What now?" is the attitude. The first one shows a hint of progressive energy and the willingness to continue working. The "What now?" shows the opposite and unfriendly attitude. God works better with the "Now What?" attitude and entrusts it with many blessings, but is against and despises the "What now?" attitude.

The "Now What?" is a trigger for good things, and an outlet for us to work out the bad stuff, and life is a lot about that, taking the good and the bad… Often life is about dealing with what is in front of you. In the movie "The Martian" the main guy says "I guarantee you that at some point, everything's gonna go south on you. And you're gonna say, 'This is it. This is how I end.' Now you can either accept that, or you can get to work." Now I wonder what God must say about our "Now What?" questions.

Reading now from Gospel of John 2: 1-11 – "On the third day there was a wedding in Cana of Galilee, and the mother of Jesus was there. 2 Jesus and his disciples had also been invited to the wedding. 3 When the wine gave out, the mother of Jesus said to him, "They have no wine." 4 And Jesus said to her, "Woman, what concern is that to you and me? My hour has not yet come." 5 His mother said to the servants, "Do whatever he tells you." 6 Now standing there were six stone water-jars for the Jewish rites of purification, each holding twenty or thirty gallons.7 Jesus said to them, "Fill the jars with water." And they filled them up to the brim. 8 He said to them, "Now draw some out, and take it to the chief steward." So, they took it. 9 When the steward tasted the water that had become wine, and did not know where it came from (though the servants who had drawn the water knew), the steward called the bridegroom 10 and said to him, "Everyone serves the good wine first, and then the inferior wine after the guests have become drunk. But you have kept the good wine until now."11 Jesus did this, the first of his signs, in Cana of Galilee, and revealed his glory; and his disciples believed in him."

First, this story is not about Jesus showing his supernatural abilities, it is about Jesus dwelling in His identity with the Father. This story is not about a son making his mother happy. It is about an adult who knows the importance of a host being able to provide to the guest.

This story is not about Jesus encouraging drunkenness, but it is about Jesus showing great concern for the wellbeing of the new couple. The Wedding at Cana is a story that demonstrates that God not only cares about your salvation from the burning flames of hell, but that God also cares about the simple things in life that bring you happiness. This story is about God answering the "Now What?" questions.

To better understand the story that we just read, I want you to see things from the perspective of Jesus. In this way, you will be able to get some insight that will be helpful to your personal life.

Don't think about the Jesus that suffers willingly on the cross, but about the Jesus in the Gospel of John who is starting his ministry. The Jesus that is perhaps living with his parents and has just begun to have enemies who hate his message. Think about the Jesus that shows up to celebrate a wedding of a friend and relative, who loves a good time and who gets invited to social events, not as a preacher or savior, but as a guest, just a mere guest.

Also, let us recognize that the Jesus of the story is still Jesus of the same essence of the Father, but is in the early stages of developing his confidence and learning his role within God's plan. To me, it is unlikely that Jesus had all knowledge, all wisdom from the beginning, but rather that the fear of the Lord and his wisdom grew stronger every day.

Having that understanding will allow us to connect with Jesus in a more natural way; Jesus struggles with what we struggle with. Jesus was tempted the way that we are being tempted. In our story, Jesus asked the question, "Now What," and God, the Father, in His infinite wisdom said, "Look within!" per our reading of the Gospel.

a. Look within: the time to act is now,
b. Look within: you have the authority,
c. Look within: God's glory is our purpose.

a. Look within: the time to act is now. What we must also realize is that the scripture says that Jesus was invited and that his mother was already there. That should be interesting to us because we should not assume that Jesus' mother was a guest also, rather, perhaps she was a host thus explaining why she was concerned about the wine.

It is interesting how there is little or no conversation between Jesus and his mother. A few ideas worth mentioning, Jesus calls Mary, "Woman," thus detaching himself from her, yet keeping the respect and the relational value between them. Jesus is claiming that his time has not yet come, and Mary like knowing something that Jesus did not know said: "Do whatever he tells you." On this occasion, Jesus receives the ultimate acknowledgment from the one that has been with him from the beginning. Mary's reaction is outstanding which finds support from the promise of the angel.

Jesus is carefully faithful to the gospel of John about his identity, but on this occasion, in faith, I believe Mary's words are not her own.

How many times to we sit around waiting for the right time to do something? How many times do we put off doing something that we feel called to, because the time is not perfect, or because you do not feel ready, but once we start it we do not know why we did not start sooner?

I believe the time is now for you to do what God is calling you to do. There is no point in waiting, and there is no benefit. Most of us have a feeling, yet we need to reaffirm one another in the love of Christ.

b. Look within: you have the authority Believing that the words of Mary "Do whatever he tells you!" are not her own but come from God the Father, who uses Mary as a messenger. We believe that Jesus has the authority and the confidence to make things happen, to show the good, excellent and perfect power of God, for his glory. To gain a better understanding of how things work, look at the scripture. The servants are doing and following everything that Jesus is requiring. Understand that Jesus is not their master. They do not need to follow Jesus' indications, but why do they do it? I believe it has to do something with where Jesus' authority comes from.

What is interesting is that the power is not only for Jesus, rather because of His love we have been given the same power. Because of our faith and because of the church, and because of Jesus Christ, you have authority also. You have the authority to do good. Because of your faith, you can perform miracles! Now I am not saying that if you touch water, the water will be turned into wine, but I am also not saying that it cannot happen.

Doing good for others is an act of God, knowing that all good comes from God. The more you are in communion with God and the more you study his words, the better you will do. You do good because you have an idea of what goodness look like, which comes from God. The more knowledge, the more prayer, the more studying you do, the better you will be able to exercise your authority.

c. Look within: God's glory ought to be our purpose. Now after the power of God had transformed the water into wine, Jesus commanded the servants to take it to the chief steward, but what is the purpose of this? And why to the chief steward and not to the bridegroom? Because Jesus did not do the good thing in order to seek His glory. The act of doing good should be enough for you and me if it were good enough for our Lord Jesus Christ.

Also, know that it would of being an embarrassment to the bridegroom for a guest to see after the care of another guest.

That's why there is a level of secrecy in this story but also because the purpose of our actions should speak about the One that gives us life, and not about ourselves. It is interesting that in this miracle, there was no prayer, there was no testimony or required answer, there was no touch. Just the willingness to do things in the name of the Father was enough.

May you remember to seek God, and surrender to God's will, in all honesty, and humbleness asking, "Now What?" questions and consider avoiding the "What Now?" attitude. May you remember that the time to act is now, that you have all authority, understanding and that your purpose in life is to honor God. Amen.

Look Outside!

What is the toughest conversation you have ever had? Perhaps it is the one with your spouse when you were let go from your job, or the time that you had to call your parents from the police department, or the one about sex with your teenager. Personally, I've had a few tough conversations, but the most difficult conversation that I ever had to have happened around 2 or 3 in the morning back in 2013. I was on call as a chaplain for the Kettering network of hospitals; I was paged to a room at the Sycamore Hospital; this was during my Clinical Pastoral Care Training.

The request came from the ICU staff, and as I remember they had a patient that might not live through the night with a DNR. I arrived at the floor, and as usual, I went to talk to the floor nurse. I remember that they were not as chatty as usual and took me directly to the room, which was in front of the nurse station. As I entered the room, the husband rushed to greet me and says, "Thank You, Father, for coming; I want you to offer prayer." I say, "Sure. What do you want me to pray for?" He says, "A miracle. I want God to heal my wife." Then we both approach the bed—You must know that as chaplain, our purpose is to care for the patient and the patient's family. We are taught to talk directly to the patient, and if not able, to find the next of kin. In our situation, it was evident.

So, I started to pray, but to my disbelief, the second I said "Amen," her heart stopped... Nurses rushed in, the husband and I take a step back, he turns around and grabs me by the shoulders. Looks at me and we make eye contact, and he says "What happened? How come your prayer didn't work. I mean, if God doesn't listen to you, why would we pay attention to me?" The Nurses look at me, like asking,

"You need help?" But nothing really happens. The husband turns around and cries like I never heard a man cry before. I don't know how much time I was in the room, but I remember asking God in prayer for the words to say something theologically sound, but I never said anything. I remember that after a while the husband said "I am thankful to God. I am grateful for our lives, and the life that I lived because of her. Thank you for your company, Padre. Thank you for staying with me, and not letting me be alone."

That was a "Now What? Look Outside" moment in my ministry. While trying to gather the courage and words from within, I realized that the encouragement and loved that the husband needed was from outside. I understand that there wasn't anything I could have said to alleviate his pain or decrease his wishes of having his wife with him, but what I did was stay in that room until the husband realized that I was there. Church, I am not the hero of the story, I am nothing but an instrument that was used to witness a miracle of God. And so, that is the toughest conversation that I ever had. I was talking to God, and God said to be quiet, and let me do the talking. Listen, and you might learn a thing or two. "Now What? Look Outside" might be a concept strange to most of you. As I said last week, "Now what?" is a question that allows you to surrender your life in worship for the Glory of the one and only.

Last week we talked about the idea that if we stop and ask God the "Now What?" question, he will reply "Look Within," because the time to act is now, you have the authority, and your purpose is my Glory, says the Lord. But this week God also says when you ask the question "Now What?" I will say "Look Outside" because God's promises will be fulfilled. People will try to bring you down and people will NOT recognize your authority.

As we read the Gospel of Luke 4: 14 - 24, our Lord Jesus tell us that His promises will be fulfilled, which means that He will come back, which means that there will be a division between those who will live an eternity without God, and those who will be welcomed into paradise forever. In lay terms, some of us will be welcomed into heaven and some of us will be sent to hell, but that's not all. Don't hit the panic button just yet. Look at all the promises that Jesus made within the scriptures. In a quick search, I could find at least 50 promises, and within a larger search, I could find almost 200.

All I am telling you is that these promises that God made a long time ago will become a reality in front of our eyes. Do you know what these promises are? Do your children know what these promises are?

If your answer is NO, then you are in a predicament. Are you going to continue avoiding these promises? Are you only going to accept the one about hell? Or are you going to start paying attention to your spiritual life? But there is a bigger question, if you are an adult and you don't care about your spiritual life, you are an adult what can I say, but what about your children and your grandchildren? Shouldn't they have the opportunity to know?

That's what I am going to say about that subject right now. If you consider Christian Education as a priority, get involved. We have great ideas, but without you, and without you bringing your children we have nothing.

They will try to take you down, look at what happened to Jesus in Luke 4: 22, when the people around Jesus said, "Isn't this Joseph's son?" which is a very polite way to remember that Jesus was the son of someone, a.k.a. another sinner, just like the next. And so, that is what people will do to you; occasionally you are trying your best to glorify God in what you do. You go around asking God "Now What

Lord?" And someone will yank your clothes and say, hey remember that you are a sinner and that you are not perfect. Bear in mind that you are no better than me, and what you do doesn't matter, because at the end nobody is perfect and you are a sinner!

And you will feel terrible and as if what you do doesn't matter and this is where you need to remember, what you do matters. Look at what we learned last week. "Now What?" you say, and the Lord replies… Look within and know that the time to act is now. You have the authority to do many things, especially if they are done to glorify God. The Lord says, look outside and know that my promises will be fulfilled, but remember that when you do my work people will try to bring you down but you have to trust my promises and trust my word. Says the Lord.

Finally, know that sometimes those close to you will not recognize your authority. They will see the goodness that you do, but they will prefer to remember your mistakes. Because no prophet is accepted in the prophet's hometown. Because people choose not to see the light, but only remember the darkness. And so, you need to be prepared and have a good foundation in God's promises and God's value of your life and Ministry.

Usually, the people that will do it are the people close to you. Usually, it is your family, your spouse and your children who will choose to remember your mistakes, and you should say that is ok. That is ok because I do not do it because of you, I do it because God is calling me to do it, and because God's promises are real I will worship his name, knowing that God is the one that has the power to judge and who chooses to give me eternal life.

May you remember to ask, "Now What Lord?"

May your call be affirmed in the knowledge that God is calling you to act now with God's authority and for God's Glory. May you remember to ask, "Now What Lord?" remembering to look outside and know that God's promises will become a reality, that people will try to bring you down and that they will not recognize your authority. May you continue the good work and the good fight. May God call you good and faithful servant. Amen.

See and Repeat

The last couple of weeks we have been talking about the difference between, "Now What?" and the almost nemesis, "What Now?" By asking "Now What?" we proclaim that God is Lord and that we serve God. "Now What?" allows us to become one with our call in Christ Jesus.

And so, in our first Sunday of our sermon series we read John 2: 1-11 and we learned that God answers our "Now What?" The question with "Look Within" because part of the answer is within us. In that answer, God is telling us that

a. The time to act is now, to do what God is calling you to do.
b. You have all authority remember that influence is from out of this world and that you are called to do amazing things.
c. The purpose of glorifying God's name in all that you do.

In our second Sunday of our sermon series, we read Luke 4: 14-24 and we asked the question again, "Now What?" and God replies, "Look outside." In that answer, God is telling us that

a. All the promises will become real, while
b. Speaking the truth people will try to bring you down, some
c. Some people will not recognize your authority, the one you got from God to do God's will.

Today is our third and final day in our sermon series, and as we meet for worship and prepare for our congregational meeting we ask the Lord, "Now What?" and God says, "See and Repeat." And we should understand this answer in the context of Jeremiah 1: 4-10.

The Scriptures says, "Now the word of the LORD came to me saying, "Before

I formed you in the womb I knew you, and before you were born I consecrated you; I appointed you a prophet to the nations." Then I said, "Ah, Lord GOD! Truly I do not know how to speak, for I am only a boy." 7 But the LORD said to me, "Do not say, 'I am only a boy'; for you shall go to all to whom I send you, and you shall speak whatever I command you. Do not be afraid of them, for I am with you to deliver you, says the LORD." Then the LORD put out his hand and touched my mouth; and the LORD said to me, "Now I have put my words in your mouth. See, today I appoint you over nations and kingdoms, to pluck up and to pull down, to destroy and to overthrow, to build and to plant."

We are children of God with an amazing prophecy. God is calling us to see what we have done (the good and the bad) and repeat (what gives God the glory). Know that we can choose to see everything and repeat everything, but there is no growth in that. So, my challenge today is to see that today is not January 31st of 2016, but today is January 31st of 2021 which is not a made-up day. Our next January 31st will be in the year 2021.

Think about our Church and our Call five years from now. What things we accomplish, what would be the struggles that we will have and the ones that we have overcome. Think about your life in this community and your relationship with the person next to you.

Think about reading the prophecy of Jeremiah in the context of our church. "Now the word of the LORD came to me saying, "Before I formed you in the womb I knew you, and before you were born I consecrated you; I appointed you a prophet to the nations." Then I said, "Ah, Lord GOD! Truly I do not know how to speak, for I am only a CHURCH." 7 But the LORD said to me, "Do not say, 'I am only a CHURCH'; for you shall go to all to whom I send you, and you shall speak whatever I command you. Do not be afraid of the WORLD, for I am with you to deliver you, says the LORD." Then the LORD put out his hand and touched OUR mouth; and the LORD said to the US, "Now I have put my words in your mouth. See, today I appoint you over nations and kingdoms, to pluck up and to pull down, to destroy and to overthrow, to build and to plant."

I want us to ask, "Now What?" And I want you to hear the answer that God has reserved for you. Perhaps God will say, see the good that you have done, forget the bad and repeat what brings me glory, growing by my spirit and by my promises. Amen.

Wait, did I read the right lesson? I mean it says here John, Gospel of

John. In this gathering of books which we call the Bible, but it doesn't sound like the Bible. I mean we just read the story of a crazy, violent person. Who is this person? Who is this Jesus and what happened to the Jesus that we know?

You know the Jesus that said love your neighbor, the one that was gentle and spoke of kindness, who taught us the concept of turning the other cheek, and said that when someone wanted to take your coat, you should also give them your shirt and finally got himself killed on behalf of the world where most people do not believe in him?

Who is this Jesus who makes a whip of cords, who becomes violent and behaves in a disorderly manner? Who is yelling at people, flipping tables possibly breaking stuff that doesn't belong to him? Is it possible that this is the same Jesus?

Well yes, it is! And that should make you feel different. You think you might know Jesus, but let me tell you Jesus has a curve ball that you have never seen, a curve ball that challenges everything that you know and that surely will give you the chills.

If you think Jesus is a puzzle and you have it all figured out, let me tell you that your puzzle isn't over until God calls you to God's presence. Our journey with Christ isn't over until God says that it is over.

I mean look at the curveball that Jesus is throwing us now.

But before I continue I want to make sure you remember something. Jesus is not throwing you a curve ball to strike you out. Jesus is your creator (your coach, your mentor, your guide) and as your coach, Jesus is throwing you a curve ball to teach you how to hit a curveball so that you may know how to hit them when life pitches against you.

In our lesson, we see that Jesus goes back to Jerusalem for the festival of the Passover. In case you don't remember, the festival of the Passover is a celebration that honors the emancipation of the people of Israel from slavery in Egypt.

Remember that this is not the first time Jesus is in Jerusalem, and this is not the first time that Jesus sees what's going on in the temple, but it is one of the last times that he would enter the temple as a common man.

We must agree that Jesus reaction is not a normal-JC-reaction. In fact, there are only one or two occasions where Jesus reacts to a situation in a very physical and human way. I say one or two occasions because it depends whether you believe there are two "cleansing of the temple" times or only one.

John describes the cleansing of the temple as occurring during the first (of three) Passover mentioned in his Gospel. Meanwhile, Matthew, Mark, and Luke all describe the temple cleansing as taking place just days before Christ's Crucifixion.

When I read the text, I see a Jesus showing his frustration in a very tangible way; there is no story, there is no quick smart answer, there is no parable in his reaction. If anything, this event just seems foolish.

Why do I say foolish? Well, Jesus has proved throughout His ministry that love is what changes the world, not violence. If Jesus knows that violence is not the best way to address a problem and still does it, that's what we call foolish.

And saying that God is capable of foolishness is not blaspheme. That is just an analysis of 1 Corinthians 1:25 "For God's foolishness is wiser than human wisdom, and God's weakness is stronger than human strength."

Reflecting on that text made me look at Jesus' actions in a different way, and made me realize that Jesus might have been foolish (making a whip and being violent), but that his actions are perfect.

Having that in mind, it allowed to me to discover that Jesus' actions teach us a lot about how we ought to behave when there is something that is bothering us within our place of worship.

The first thing that comes to mind is making sure that people know that you are upset and that what is bothering you is important.

Church, I am not saying that you should make a whip and enter the church and start flipping tables when you are upset because of something that Rev. Lindsey or I, or Peggy or someone at the church said or did or didn't do.

What I am saying is that you need the courage and the appropriate tools to get people's attention, because that was what the whip was for. If you read the scriptures, you read that

Jesus had a whip, NOT that Jesus was whipping people. Do you see the difference?

I mean have you been in a public market where there is livestock and people are doing business out loud? I am sorry, but you are not going to be effective if you go and talk in a soft voice and start saying please and thank you.

There is a time for everything, and for Jesus, this was a time to make people pay attention. So, is there anything that is bothering you about our church, and are you effectively communicating your disappointment?

Which takes me to the second thing that we ought to learn when communicating a disappointment—make sure that you are telling the right people; the people that can make a difference or can improve the situation.

In the text, who is Jesus talking to? Is Jesus talking to his disciples (people that have nothing to do with what is troubling Him), or is Jesus talking directly to the people who are part of the issue?

When there is a situation in a church that is bothering you, please let us make sure that we are talking directly to the people that can address the situation and make a difference.

Jesus wasn't talking to his disciples about the situation because the disciples didn't have anything to do with it. Talking to his disciples would have been like gossiping which brings a lot of things, but not changes and not an improvement.

We are called to build each other up, learn from one another, not gossip about one another and share our disagreement with one another without seeking improvement. There is a difference between talking to the people that can help address the situation and talking to the people that can only listen and dwell with you in your disagreement.

Finally, and this might be the hardest to do and understand. Be patient with one another and do not expect for the issue to be fixed immediately.

Remember that we are dealing with one another and we are humans, and how we present our case or request and how we tolerate one another is half of the battle.

Jesus' request didn't change anything at first. If anything, it got him into trouble first. Here is where Jesus shows us how to be patient and be agents of change within the church. Jesus spoke in truth and was constantly asking people to change.

Why do you or I give up so easily when there is something that upsets us? It is ugly and horrible how easy is to quit church rather than to deal with each other.

Quitting on the church because the church is not doing what we want is not something that we learned from Gospels. What we learn from the good news of Jesus Christ is to dwell within one another despite our differences for the Glory of God.

May we learn to find the right tools to communicate our disagreement effectively, without violence and hate. May we learn to trust one another and to not be afraid to express our differences. May we learn to be patient with one another and ourselves and to not quit in the life and hope that we find in our community. Amen.

The Good Shepherd

There is a theme between the two scriptures that we read this morning. I am sure that such suggestion is no surprise to any of you. After all, I have the title of Teaching Elder, Preacher, and Ordained Minister of the Word and Sacrament. Part of my vocation is to organize worship in a way that makes sense, remains current and is attractive to members and our guest. But above all that my vocation gives the Glory to God in every prayer, song or scripture that is read and preached.

You can say it is a win-win situation for me. I am a man entrusted to perform one of the most beautiful tasks on planet earth—Lead worship. Some people will compare us ministers as the shepherds and the congregation as our flock, but I have always struggled with that idea.

I am sure that most of you have heard such analysis before. Ministers and congregations being shepherds and flock, right? But I know better than to assume things, so let me see your hand if you have ever contemplated or heard that there is a relationship between ministers and the congregation, as shepherds and the flock?

Now, that I have you engaged and smiling and giggling, allow me to ask for your participation one more time. Have you ever contemplated the biblical relationship between the church as the head and Jesus Christ as the real shepherd? Read Scripture!

This passage is one of the reasons why I struggle with being compared to a Shepherd now that I am a minister.

Indeed, Jesus is the Good Shepherd. In fact, the Christian church has traditionally observed this Fourth Sunday of Easter as the

"Good Shepherd Sunday!"

Personally, I always look forward to this Sunday.

I mean Jesus just said that "I am The Good Shepherd." Who am I even to consider having a part of such a title? But studying and preparing this sermon allowed me to understand why it is an edifying concept.

Let me begin by saying that I enjoy this reading from the Gospel of John because it is simple. I like it because it is powerful. I like it because it is human. But I love it because it is provocative.

Jesus says, "I am the Good Shepherd," and before we go any further let me give you a helpful insight when reading the Bible—pay close attention every time that Jesus says, "I AM." You might find things like… Jesus is "The Good Shepherd," but that does not make Him the only kind of shepherd there is right?

The scriptures are telling us that there are at least a few other kinds of shepherd like, "only for the money shepherd," or the "runaway shepherd."

Something important to remember is that the "Shepherd" is an analogy of behavior that Jesus displayed many times, even after his crucifixion. It was an analogy that people could easily relate to. Remember that Jesus never had the profession of a shepherd; Jesus only had the behavior of one. But what do I mean? Well it is quite simple.

Sheep are different than any other livestock; shepherd leads sheep, but they are never pushed. Just like Jesus would lead us into believing, but will never push us into believing.

As Disciples of Christ, we can attempt to behave like Jesus would. I understand now that because my master was, I can consider being one myself. Not because of me, but because of him.

We can say that when we lead others, help each other reach our spiritual goals, or when we care for each other in any physical or spiritual way, we have the behavior that looks a lot like the behavior that made Jesus "The Good Shepherd."

I am more comfortable with the idea of being a shepherd. In ministry, we have that virtue and commitment to be shepherds as Christ was. But this deeper understanding of accepting being a shepherd like Christ brought something challenging to my heart.

That virtue and commitment are not only for ministers. Which lead me to realize that we have a concern of titles, tags or nicknames. Not talking about a power struggle with titles, or graffiti tags on our walls or bullying each other with nicknames.

In our church, we have Teaching Elders, Ruling Elders, Deacons. Also, we have Teachers, Engineers, Doctors, Nurses, Accountants, Designers, Husband, Wives, Students; all these are titles. In our church, we have people with tags, not talking about clothing tags or anything like that. I am talking about people who care so much about a cause, a foundation, program or organization that they label themselves pro something or against something.

In our church, we have people with nicknames, people who are recognized by something that they do, something that has become part of their identity and sometimes even their name. For example, Sandy Nichols sometimes calls me, "Hello Church" or "Good morning Church."

Titles, tags or nicknames, they announce a part of your identity. And Church that is great. The issue is that sometimes these things limit our potential and give us barriers that are hard to put down.

Church, we need titles to talk about our labor, we need tags to identify what we value or what causes we defend, we need nicknames to speak of our familiarity and knowledge of each other.

We need it because we are humans and because our understanding of each other is limited, but you cannot let those things completely define who you are or what you do in life and your church because God is calling you to be more than what you are right now.

It doesn't matter if you are a youth, age 16 getting ready to go on the mission trip or a 69-year-old looking to retire or an 83-year-old enjoying life after work. Being a Christian is an evolution process where God is always raising the bar and calling you to improve.

How can you improve and help your church improve? Well, I thought you would never ask. We can improve by participating more in activities of leadership and investing our time more and more in things that Glorify God.

We can improve by challenging and improving what we are already doing if you are in a program by talking talk to whoever is in charge of that program. See how you can serve and improve the life of those who are participating in the program with you. Do not get stuck doing all the work yourself, ask for help. Do not get stuck doing it all. Ask for help. Start by asking your minister to help you do it and find others that can also help.

Church, we cannot continue thinking that in church only the leaders lead. Church, everyone has a purpose, talents and the encouragement of the Holy Spirit to achieve great things. I might be the minister, but I am sure that the Holy Spirit also talks to you. Do not be a sheep only, be a shepherd and a sheep

You do not need titles; you do not need to have a tag to be involved in something meaningful; you do not need a nickname to work with the youth or to show to the congregation your gifts and talents. The worst thing that a church can do is to only let a few do all the work. Church, that should not happen in a church like ours where there is so much potential, so many people with the abilities to teach.

May we help each other to be both sheep and shepherds. May we discover our potential as rightful children of the covenant knowing that leadership does not come from titles, tags or nicknames, rather it comes from the love and encouragement of the Holy Spirit. All Honor and Glory to the One that save us. Amen.

Happy Birthday, Church

Back in Ohio, I had a great group of friends who I used to play softball with. We played every Monday and every Tuesday. Sometimes we would play on Thursdays, and sure sometimes we played Fridays. We would play weekend tournaments and all-nighters. By the all-nighters, I mean tournaments that you play starting around 6 or 7 pm and you will be playing until about 4 or 5 in the morning, if you were lucky.

One time we played until 7 am "the next day," but we decided to flip a coin to see who would take 1st place because nobody could play anymore. We were so tired, but it felt so good.

Anyway, winning was never the question; the question was who want to be the last out. Winning was never the question; the question was, when is the next tournament.

We were 10, sometimes we were 11. We were not the best of athletes, but on the field, we knew each other, and that means the world. We would win or lose a game all by ourselves.

I now understand that it was never about softball, it was about something more significant than what we were doing together. I do have to say that I was often the responsible one and that our IQ would drop 20 points the minute we would get together. But we worked like a well-oiled hitting machine.

We had our language; it was a thing of beauty. What do I mean? Well, one time Jake the "J" on the left field made a difficult catch for the last

out of the inning. The catch was a dive, and he caught the ball with the top of the glove. The minute that Jake raised his hand I screamed "Ice Cone!" and everyone just died laughing... Let me explain. Normally when something like that happened, you're supposed to yell "Snow Cone." But since that day, the team would never say "Snow Cone" they would just say "Ice Cone." And so, it was never funny to anybody else, but it was funny to us, and that was all that mattered.

You see, language can take you places and can be everything to a group. And that is the first thing I wanted to talk to you about. Look at what happens to the group of the story in Genesis. Read Genesis 11: 1-9 and look at what happens when God took away their ability to speak the same language. Also, remember that language isn't just the words that you use to speak.

Language it is anything and everything that you have between two people that know each other. A look, a smirk, an inside joke. Think about your significant other, about your close friends, and now imagine that someone wiped out the way you communicate with them. Sure, you can learn to communicate again but is never going to be the same.

Which makes me consider the second thing I wanted to talk to you about today. How do you create a language with someone? Do you do it by choosing to have a language? Sure. But what is the best way to get a language with someone or a group if it is not by spending time together?

In Genesis and Acts we see it. In Genesis, we read that the group migrated from the east, and you know that thing doesn't happen over a day, and in Acts, we read that they were all together in one place. So, the idea of spending time together is crucial to understand how amazing things begin to happen.

The people that were together on that day in Acts 2 are not strangers that decided just to get together one day. It was an important reunion to celebrate the Shavuot which is one of the three great festivals of Judaism. This festival is a loud, energetic, and joyful feast of the dedication of the first fruits. So, it is no accident that these friends were together. It was with the intention of remembering Jesus Christ, as that day marked the 50th day, or Seven Weeks, since Jesus Death and Resurrection.

This festival, called Shavuot, is the festival of the First Fruits of the Harvest which is a God-Incidence because more than anything, Shavuot is the celebration of the giving of the Torah, the Ten Commandments from Mount Sinai. Just as for Jews the exodus revelation signals the birth of the chosen people of God. For Christians, the Pentecost narrative signals the birth of the church.

So, Happy Birthday Church! It was no accident that you are here. And because it is your Birthday, God continues to celebrate with you and continues to support us and give us gifts.

Which makes me consider the third thing I wanted to talk to you about today. So, I read John 14: 25-27 "I have said these things to you while I am still with you. 26 But the Advocate, the Holy Spirit, whom the Father will send in my name, will teach you everything, and remind you of all that I have said to you. 27 Peace I leave with you; my peace I give to you. I do not give to you as the world gives. Do not let your hearts be troubled, and do not let them be afraid."

In here, you hear Jesus talking while he was still with his disciples. He was presenting a very special gift which is being addressed from the Father to the church, in order to do some useful things: to teach, and to remind us.

With the understanding that Jesus not only leaves his peace, but He also gives it to us as a gift. Jesus' peace is not just something that he forgot to take with him on his way to heaven. Jesus knew that we were going to need it, so he decided to give it to us.

And because we are who we are, and because Jesus is who Jesus is. Jesus reminds us that His gifts are very special gifts and that there is nothing that this world can offer you—fame, money, prestige, power, etc.—that is better than what Jesus gave us.

So why are our hearts troubled and full of panic? Why are we always afraid? And why does all this matter?

Because we forget, we need a constant reminder that we have all our priorities wrong… but Mario how is that? Well, isn't the church the afterthought? Isn't it that during a busy weekend with extracurricular activities, the first thing that we want to cancel is Church? It might come as a surprise to the world, but the church is not the building. If the church is not the building if the church is not what we do or the fancy things we say, what is Church? Church is the relationship between you and you. Between them and you. Between those outside and us. Church is between you, the new confirmation class, Rev. Lindsey, the Choir, Sue and Miss Doris and Peggy Surdam, and Presbytery, and the neighbor that you don't like and everyone else in between.

Church is about relationship in the unifying Grace of God. Because of that relationship today we have the confirmation class lead worship. Since we've started to meet, the first thing that I wanted to tell them is that the Church is not these beautiful windows and these walls with a tall ceiling. Church is the desire between two people in the name of God to seek to love one another despite the differences, not out of their strength but with the eternal strength of God.

Church is the people that you see in around you.

May you remember that when you are saying "no" to church, you are saying "no" to one another, and today I want you to consider saying "yes" to each other. Yes. Amen.

Since You Called Me to Be with You!

I have been giving thanks to the Lord our God whom we worship, for taking me to such a place where, once you learn how to spell it and how to say it; it gets stuck in your heart.

In fact, a year ago today, I made the announcement on Facebook about how I was blessed to start my journey into ministry with you. It was an exciting time, and it is still an exciting time. It is good to give thanks and praise to each other for the work that we do in Jesus Christ. You would not be the only one. In fact, the Apostle Paul does the same thing.

Let us now pay attention to the word of God found in the letter to the Ephesians 1: 15-23, listen to God's word.

I have heard of your faith in the Lord Jesus and your love[a] toward all the saints, and for this reason 16 I do not cease to give thanks for you as I remember you in my prayers. 17 I pray that the God of our Lord Jesus Christ, the Father of glory, may give you a spirit of wisdom and revelation as you come to know him, 18 so that, with the eyes of your heart enlightened, you may know what is the hope to which he has called you, what are the riches of his glorious inheritance in the saints, 19 and what is the immeasurable greatness of his power for us who believe, according to the working of his great power. 20 God[b] put this power to work in Christ when he raised him from the dead and seated him at his right hand in the heavenly places, 21 far above all rule and authority and power and dominion, and above every name that is named, not only in this age but also in the age to come. 22 And he has put all things under his feet and has made him the head over all things for the church, 23 which is his body, the fullness of him who fills all in all.

I believe it was joy that the Apostle Paul felt when he elaborated these words of celebration on behalf of the church of the Ephesians.

Paul was impressed because their faith and love were evidence of their participation in the great work of God, evidence being the key word. Evidence is a big deal for us human beings. We are always seeking evidence.

What do we understand as evidence? It is the "available body of facts or information indicating whether a belief or proposition is true or valid." Considering evidence is something automatic; "A" plus "B" equals "C" kind of thing. Through evidence, we can make assessments and make judgment calls. Evidence is at the center of our sense, logic, and awareness.

After I got married, and while dealing with the United States Citizenship and Immigration Services, they asked for evidence of our marriage. Pictures, statements, our love letters—Evidence!

But I am not here to impart a doctrine of Evidence! My goal was to remind you how significant Evidence is for us as a human being.

Going back to our scripture, Paul was very impressed by the evidence of faith and love that the church of Ephesians was providing.
Perhaps, the apostle Paul was as impressed with the church in Ephesians as I was impressed with the evidence of faith and love that the First Presbyterian Church offered me when I was considering accepting the call that you were offering.

I do not know if you have paid attention to the things that you as a congregation have accomplished. Our church has done a lot for the Glory of God and for the world to know about the good news of Jesus.

Last week during my retreat for Early Ministry Institute, people were delighted and joyful to hear about all the things that you have accomplished for the glory of God as a church.

It is no lie; the evidence that we can show about our ministries and dedication for the Glory of God is vast and impressive. I know that the creation of my position is part of that evidence. My position was created in pursuit of what God is calling you to be and do. So, we ought to rejoice and remember that when there are churches in our presbytery that are closing and struggling to keep their staff. You decided in faith that you were going to call an Associate Pastor.

So, What Now—remember?

Last week while I was at the Early Ministry Institute, there was a question that put several things into perspective. The question was—If your church were to close its doors tomorrow, what do you think the community would miss the most? Not you, not the members of the church, but your community. What do you think the community would miss the most?

Is it the building? The pretty weddings? The Dobson Hall? The offices for the Skaneateles Music Festival? Or the Montessori school or the Wednesday Moms and Kids program?

The question has no easy answer. As a church, we cannot control what the community would miss the most. That is, in fact, the work of the Holy Spirit. Sure, there are things that we can control and oversee, but not 100%

In reality, the purpose of the question is not to force us to find an answer, rather to give us a reality check. The outcome of our actions it is not up to us, but it's up to the Holy Spirit. But that does not mean that we cannot try to answer the question.

Our possible answer might be. Our church will not close because I am a member of my church. By the Glory of God, I would never let this church close its doors. My country needs this church, my community needs this church, and my family needs this church. But at the end, when all is said and done, what I want you to really say and know is "I need this Church!" Because you need this Church I want you to do what the Apostle Paul did. I want you to give thanks to all the Evidence that, as a church we can provide. But I also want you to realize that Evidence is a term, a signal or an event of the past, and as a church, we cannot live in the past.

It is good to remember the efforts of coming together to build an addition to the church, to organize the Presbyterian Manor and the John Dau Foundation, to help to create and support the Ecumenical Food Pantry, and to call an Associate Pastor it is all great for the glory of God.

But I also want you to do the following: Giving thanks is the first thing. Always give thanks, the second one is to continue to ask, "Now What?" But understand that our purpose is not to simply pursue our next project or program.

The church is not Bob, the builder. It is not about task after task. It is not about asking yourself or asking the person next to you. It is not about asking your Pastor or your Associate Pastor or the chair of your committee or board or the Session. It is about "I pray[ing] that the God of our Lord Jesus Christ, the Father of glory, may give [us] a spirit of wisdom and revelation as [we] come to know him." Ephesians 1: 17

Now Church, can you see? It is not about us answering the questions, but is about God, with the Holy Spirit guiding us to the answer.

I want us as a church to ask, "Now What?" in prayer!

I want us to become a church of prayer, a Church that is active, a Church that is a "Martha," but that can also be a "Mary."

I want us to continue working on the evidence of love and faith, but I also want us to gather in prayer to ask, "Now What, Lord?"

Church, when all is said and done, I want us to pray. I want us to invite the Holy Spirit and for the Holy Spirit to dwell in us and through us.

May we learn to recognize our journey and to find joy in all the things that we have accomplished, realizing that it is not a race or competition.

May we gather in adoration knowing that we are a church that knows how to work, plan, and build ministries for the benefit of others

But may we also remember that we cannot remain in the memory of the things that we have achieved, rather we should live and die seeking the path to the glory of God. Amen.

Between a Rock and a Hard Place

Do you remember that beautiful morning? It was sunny outside, there was a gentle breeze, and the birds were singing all in tune, but the only thing you wanted to do was to stay in bed and wait for the final blow. And you wondered when the string of bad things was going to end?

Have you ever been stuck between a rock and a hard place? A time where you did not see a way out and your troubles were calling? Well I have. And I am sure that most of you can remember times such as those. And on those days, it is when I read the following scripture:

"And the crowd came together again so that they could not even eat. 21 When his family heard it, they went out to restrain him, for people were saying, "He has gone out of his mind." 22 And the scribes who came down from Jerusalem said, "He has Beelzebul, and by the ruler of the demons he casts out demons." 23 And he called them to him, and spoke to them in parables, "How can Satan cast out Satan? 24 If a kingdom is divided against itself, that kingdom cannot stand. 25 And if a house is divided against itself, that house will not be able to stand. 26 And if Satan has risen against himself and is divided, he cannot stand, but his end has come. 27 But no one can enter a strong man's house and plunder his property without first tying up the strong man; then indeed the house can be plundered. 28 "Truly I tell you, people will be forgiven for their sins and whatever blasphemies they utter; 29 but whoever blasphemes against the Holy Spirit can never have forgiveness but is guilty of an eternal sin"— 30 for they had said, "He has an unclean spirit." 31 Then his mother and his brothers came; and standing outside, they sent to him and called him. 32 A crowd was sitting around him; and they said to him, "Your mother and your brothers and sisters are outside, asking for you." 33 And he replied, "Who are my mother and my brothers?" 34 And looking at those who sat around him, he said,

"Here are my mother and my brothers! 35 Whoever does the will of God is my brother and sister and mother." Mark 3: 20 -35

Jesus Christ on that day was stuck between a rock and a hard place. Can you see it? Jesus was dealing with some things that would affect his ministry, his family, his disciples, the people that were in the temple, and especially us!

Now, let me share with you a bit of the background of the story that we just heard. Between verses 1 to 19 of chapter 3 of the Gospel of Mark, Jesus healed and preached to a huge crowd and called by name all his VID. Remember what VID means? Very Important Disciples, Judas included.

So, as you can see, that is why the crowd, the multitude, came back together again because they were already there. And it says that "They" meaning Jesus and His group of disciples, didn't even have time to eat (or rest!).

Spiritual worship and praise take a lot of energy; there is mental fatigue and stress. Most people don't know this, but by the time Sunday is over, most ministers and worship leaders are looking to decompress.

So, I can tell you that without any doubt that Jesus was running on fumes at this point. Jesus didn't have time to take care of his human needs, like taking a break and eating any food, before the "Rock and the Hard Place" pushed forward at the worst possible time.

You might be wondering what is the "Rock and the Hard Place" of the story. Well, they have a lot to do with "Who is responsible for my house?" If you read Mark 3:21 you see that

Jesus' family was coming to get Jesus and take him home because they thought, "who is responsible for my house?" Well, not Jesus. Jesus is going crazy and is going to get himself killed and his family in trouble.

It was like Jesus was that kid playing rough at the park and his brothers and mother were coming to get him after hearing a neighbor complain. I just imagine Mary saying, "Oh wait until I see him!" or the classic "Wait until Daddy gets home."

On the other hand, the scribes, who are technically the scholars, the academia, the professors, the go-to guys for scripture, the people with a Ph.D. of the time, are calling Jesus Beelzebul. I mean they are calling Jesus prince of evil, Lord over demons and spirits.

If you ask them the question "Who is responsible for my house" talking now about the sanctuary, their answer will be, "We are" because this man called Jesus is the devil himself.

That, my dear church, is what we can call the "Rock and the Hard Place." Jesus is annoyed and frustrated by the people who should know best. They are asking a good question but coming up with the wrong answer.

I mean his family, especially his mother. The one that talked to the angel, the one that knew beyond any doubt that Jesus was Emmanuel! How could she possibly forget to believe that the right thing to do was to take him home and treat him like a child that is misbehaving?

Then you have the people who are the leaders of the time. The ones that know and interpreted the scriptures and lead people in worship to honor God. How is that these people get it so wrong that they call him prince of darkness instead of the prince of salvation?

I mean, they didn't just make a wrong turn or a common mistake. They are so wrong that Jesus says, "that their Sin will never be forgotten." That is how wrong they got it.

And so, Jesus takes this opportunity to teach us what is the thing to do when we find ourselves between a "Rock and a Hard Place." How is it that we need to answer the question, "Who oversees my house?"

The one thing that you must contemplate is that the question of this morning is not directed toward the house with the roof over your head where you live. But it is directed towards the house where your soul or spirit lives.

Honor God with your body (1 Corinthians 6:19-20). God created our bodies, Jesus Christ, redeemed them, and the Holy Spirit indwells within us. This makes our body the very temple of the Holy Spirit of God. Your body is a temple, a temple that sometimes is between a rock and a hard place.

The first thing that Jesus does is to ask simple. Clarify the question!

The "how can Satan cast out Satan?" is a clarifying question that allows the criticizer to know that Jesus took what they said very seriously and that they now have the undivided attention of Jesus. The purpose behind this is to make sure that everything is not a big misunderstanding. It is to make sure that every possibility has been exhausted, and that all things have been addressed properly.

Asking a clarifying question allows us to illustrate and paint a clear picture of the situation at hand. It allows us to consider the facts and to see if you had missed anything.

Did you get in trouble at school? Or, did you get a memo at work? Are you fighting with your spouse? Before asking anything else, make what you heard is correct, and it is not a misunderstanding.

Which takes us to the second thing...

Take the time to explain your action or thinking process. Do not assume anything! Use reason and above all remain calm.

Jesus is very upset at this point! They just called him the worst thing that you could call him, and he doesn't lose it. Jesus took the time to hear their comments and their accusations.

There is something about remaining calm in a situation of stress while taking your time to formulate your response. We are called to "all things should be done decently and in order." 1 Corinthians 14:40

I ask you my dear church, what is the purpose or the benefit of losing all decency and act like a brute during chaos? Is it not true that things could always get worse? Is it not true that a fire can burn more if it is mistreated?

How many times does a reaction cause more harm than good? Is it not better to act rather than to react? Do you know that reacting might be faster, but it is acting without thinking?

Finally, know and recognize your priorities. Adapt, regulate and rearrange your main concern to fit your needs and address the situation at hand.

After dealing with the scribes, scholars and ancient Ph.D. people, Jesus redirects his attention. His mother and his siblings are looking to yank him out of the meeting place, and Jesus is bold on his answer. Jesus' reply is still very uncomfortable to me. It does not matter how many times I read it and how much I understand it.

Jesus decides to show His priorities to the congregation saying that the people that are looking for Him are not his family, but that his family is the people that does God's will.

In all reality, Mary and the others were looking for Jesus, meaning that they were not with Jesus from the beginning. If Jesus says that His family is the one doing God's will and since His relatives are not included in that bunch, it means that His family was not participating at the time in Jesus' ministry.

Now, it is not that Jesus didn't consider them family anymore or that

Jesus was ashamed of them or did not believe their relationship was important. What Jesus said was that his relationship with the Father was more important than his relationship with them. Church, that is a cookie that it is not easy to swallow. The implications of Jesus have huge ramifications to us.

Knowing this from the perspective of a soon-to-be-Father is hard and mind-blowing. I have the opportunity to have a child. I am being entrusted with his life and his future. But God is reminding me today that my child it is not more important than my relationship with God. In the order of priorities—God is first. Again, that it is a struggle but one that we must understand and comprehend.

Regarding the question "Who is responsible for my house?" the answer is that you are responsible for the house that God gave you. You can call it your house because God gave you too!

And when the time comes and you are hurting, and you are down without energy, and you feel that your strength and spirit are broken, remember this scripture.

Remember to ask clarifying questions, making sure that the struggles are not a misapprehension or a misunderstanding.

Remember to act (use your senses, activate them with prayer) and avoid reacting to the bad things in life. Be patient, always remembering to behave in a decent way and orderly fashion.

Remember that during chaos we need to keep our eyes in our God Almighty, creator of the heavens and earth. Who is our number one priority. Amen

Who's Your Father?

One of the many identities that God has demonstrated since the beginning of our relationship is the identity of a Father. With today being Father's Day it shouldn't be a surprise that we are touching on the subject. The challenge before us today is not to simply understand that God is like a Father, but much more. It is important for you to be aware of this because "God as a Father" is an idea that has been engraved in our heart, but is an idea that can also harm us as it is an idea that creates boundaries to an entity that knows no boundaries.

God is like a father, yet God isn't simply a Father. God is more than that. If you only see God as a Father, and you believe God only plays that role, you are doing yourself a disfavor.

First Corinthians 13 says not only something about Love but also about growing up. When I was a child, I spoke, understood and thought like one, but when I became an adult thing changed.

We must remember, know, and recognize that the best way to know more about the Father is to know more about the Son— Whatever Jesus is, God is—Say it with me.

Thanks to the Son, we can say that God "the Father" is also an Interrupting God. A disrupting entity, and perhaps an agitator against the darkness of this world. You see in Genesis 1, the darkness was happy being dark, yet God came to disrupt darkness and brought light to this reality. God is not only a Father, but God is a force against the conformity and the indifference of people. Want evidence? Look at our story in the Gospel, is it outrageous?

Read Luke 8: 26-29 and see there is a man. A man that is alone, naked, unpredictable, violent. He is a gentile! A man that coexists with demons living in the midst of darkness, surrounded by death.

Now, imagine that a man is not a man, but visualize that a man is all of mankind. A man is not a stranger; a man is you, and I. And we ask Jesus, "What have you to do with me, Jesus, Son of the highest God? I beg you, do not torment me?" But it is not us that speak, rather it is something else. Reading now the continuation of our Gospel story as it is found in Luke 8: 29-33a, changing the word Man, to Mankind for the purpose of identification.

"For Jesus had commanded the unclean spirit to come out of mankind. (For many times, it had seized them; Mankind was kept under guard and bound with chains and shackles, but mankind would break the bonds and be driven by the demons into the wild.) Jesus then asked them, "What is your name?" Humanity said, "Legion"; for many demons had entered them. They begged Jesus not to order them to go back into the abyss. Now there on the hillside, a large herd of swine was feeding, and the demons begged Jesus to let them enter these. So, Jesus gave them permission. Then the demons came out of the humanity and entered the swine…"

Indeed, there is a battle out there. A battle that some of us are aware of, but the grand majority are too busy licking their wounds to realize what is happening. A battle between demons and angels, between God and Satan. God has given us the victory, but the devil is still around causing harm before the final judgment.

What is happening? is God in the persona of the Son, acting on behalf of one person but for the benefit of all. This is the second time that I restate a scripture passage by switching a word in English for the purpose of the association. But you have to understand that the switch is not arbitrary. By my vows of ordination and I am prohibited from playing with the words found in the scripture to fit what I want to say or for my purpose. I am allowed in this case because of the fullness of the original text in Greek. The switch between "Man" and "Mankind" is possible because of the original text that is written in Greek

In Greek, the word "man" or "Mankind" and "People" is Anthropos, which can be used for male or female, or generically to include all human individuals. An example where the same word is used is in Matthew 4: 19 "'Come, follow me' Jesus said, and I will send you out to fish for people." So again, what is happening is God in the persona of the Son, acting on behalf of one person but for the benefit of all.

God is an interrupting God; God likes to disrupt the false harmony and fabricated realities that we live in. Let me show again how God continues to do that in our story. Reading the rest of our story in the Gospel of Luke 8: 33-39

When the swineherds saw, what had happened, they ran off and told it in the city and the country. Then people came out to see what had happened, and when they came to Jesus, they found the man from whom the demons had gone sitting at the feet of Jesus, clothed and in his right mind. And they were afraid. Those who had seen it told them how the one who had been possessed by demons had been healed. Then all the people of the surrounding country of the Gerasenes asked Jesus to leave them; for they were seized with great fear. So, he got into the boat and returned. The man from whom the demons had gone begged that he might be with him; but Jesus sent him away, saying, "Return to your home, and declare how much God has done for you." So, he went away, proclaiming throughout the city how much Jesus had done for him.

If you pay attention to our story, you see that this man was not alone; there were obviously others around him that had a successful life with freedom and stability.

These were people who had the willingness to put this person in chains and shackles, but they didn't have the willingness to care for him. Everybody knew of the needs of this person, but they didn't care until God came to interrupt the harmony that this person had across Galilee. God disrupted their reality to bring news of salvation.

The awesome power of God can be difficult to comprehend, especially in the context of ordinary daily life. Yet that power, while beyond our human frame of reference, can transform lives. God will come and touch our lives, but it might be in a way that we do not like, or we do not understand. At this point, I could tell you why Jesus allowed the demons to go to the swine, and not just to the abyss. And we can talk about the economic and political ramifications of the actions of God in this story.

At this point, I can also share with you how being afraid played an important role in our story and how this man became one of the many missionaries across Galilee.

We can talk about how God cares about you, about the immigrant, the widow, and the orphan, about the neighbor and your enemy more than he cares about your swine.

But I find God interrupting again, to tell us that God does not interrupt for interrupting, but God interrupts our lives because that is the only way that God can tell us…

The plans I have for you," declares the LORD, "plans to prosper you and not to harm you, plans to give you hope and future. 12 Then you will call on me and come and pray to me, and I will listen to you. 13 You will seek me and find me when you seek me with all your heart. 14 You will find me," declares the LORD, "and will bring you back from captivity. [a] I will gather you from all the nations and places where I have banished you," declares the LORD, "and will bring you back to the place from which I carried you into exile."

With such promises, who cares for a few swine? Amen.

The Gift of Fear

Fear is a real thing... I read in an article of Psychology Today that fear is an emotional reaction, which causes our brain, organ functions and behavior to perform in a different way. But it seems that everyone is against being afraid. Now, I am not trying to oversimplify the emotion or concept of fear.

What I want is for us to understand that fear is not going anywhere so we might as well learn, understand and accept as much as we can about it. If fear is just an emotion, why are we so afraid of being afraid?

Fear is an emotion that most of the world likes to avoid, but today I would like to encourage you to welcome fear into your life. But there is a catch. Our challenge is to welcome Intelligent Fear and pray to God that you do not inherit Unintelligent Fear.

What is Intelligent Fear? Let us remember our Old Testament scripture.

Read Deuteronomy 31: 1 - 8

In our scripture, we find Moses, who is addressing the people of Israel. His message? He is no longer able to lead them. Moses is no longer able to lead but not because of his first statement—Being a 120—because leadership has nothing to do with age. You can be young and lead, and you can be older and still lead. Leadership has nothing to do with age, but it has everything to do with Moses' second statement. That part that says, "The Lord said: 'You shall not cross the Jordan.'"

Now pay attention to the tone of Moses in the Scripture. When we read it, do you consider that Moses is freaking out? Is he using the panic button? Do you think Moses is afraid?

I think Moses is afraid, but his fear in an Intelligent Fear. You can always tell when you are acting with intelligent fear because despite your emotions, you are moving forward and putting the needs of others before your own.

You can tell when you are acting with Intelligent Fear when you are enabling and encouraging the growth of faith of others, and the fulfillment of their call, their family ties, and association.

You can tell when you are acting with Intelligent Fear if your actions lead to your goal, which would benefit you and those around you.

You can tell when you are acting with Intelligent Fear when your actions develop positive change and produce joy in your heart.

You can tell when you are acting with Intelligent Fear when you are paying attention to the peace of God, the teaching of Jesus Christ and the company of the Holy Spirit.

But what about Unintelligent Fear? Let us now read Luke 10: 38 - 42

"38As Jesus and his disciples were on their way, he came to a village where a woman named Martha opened her home to him. 39 She had a sister called Mary, who sat at the Lord's feet listening to what he said. 40 But Martha was distracted by all the preparations that had to be made. She came to him and asked, "Lord, don't you care that my sister has left me to do the work by myself? Tell her to help me!" 41 "Martha, Martha," the Lord answered, "you are worried and upset about many things, 42 but few things are needed—or indeed only one. [a] Mary has chosen what is better, and it will not be taken away from her."

If you pay attention to the behavior of Martha within our scripture, you will see Unintelligent Fear. She was distracted, demanding attention and acknowledgment, working during worry and sadness.

Please note that it was not Jesus who started the conversation with Martha, but it was Martha who started the conversation with Jesus.

How many of us just want God to do what we want when we want it? How many of us are paying attention to Jesus and His call, His teachings, and His encouragement? How many of us are afraid because we are too busy with our plans, our agenda?

Church, our call is not to simply be afraid, but our call is to be afraid with a purpose, us not being that purpose. Us not seeking instant gratification and personal glory.

The world, the news, our government and sometimes our neighbors are telling us to be afraid, to prepare for the worst, to do things that are unintelligent such as being afraid of people that look different than you, to not help the strangers, to curse and condemn those who have a different system of beliefs. The world is telling you to use your brain and behave in fear, as if you were alone.

But the church, the Bible, the parables, the teaching and the grace of God is telling you to be afraid, but of other things: Be afraid of hate, be afraid of racist thoughts and behavior, be afraid of the separation between you and your neighbor, and be afraid of walking by a person in need and looking the other way. Be afraid of homophobia, xenophobia and any other behavior that past or future that encourages Unintelligent Fear and the possible separation between human beings because of what makes them irreplaceable.

We would do well to remember that True Wisdom comes from the Lord Proverbs 2:6 and James 3:13 --- that is why I call it Intelligent Fear. Unintelligent fear comes from our ideas and own perspectives.

We must take fear as a gift, but only the Intelligent Fear. And we should receive the Unintelligent Fear as the ugly sweater that we get around the Holidays: say thank you, yet put it some place, never to see it again.

Perhaps this does not make sense to you, but an example might help. I am planning to go to Colombia soon. These travel plans are special because I am traveling with Mel and Dante. This is only the second time for Mel, but the first for Dante. Now the link between Mel and I is strong. We entered into a covenant that is binding us into eternity. But with my son, the link goes beyond any covenant. It is something that can only be understood in the complexity of the Trinity and relationship between father and son.

Unintelligent Fear is telling me not to take my son and my wife to my birthplace because it is a third-world country where something bad might happen. Yet Intelligent Fear is telling me that I should be afraid of not taking my son and my wife to Colombia.

Both fears are real. One of them is pushing me into a corner and making me react against it, as if I was ashamed of my culture or afraid of the place where I come from. The other one is pushing me to go forward and asking me to take a risk in the name of something worthy such as my culture and the love of my family, who are the people that instructed me while I was young so I would not depart from God in my adulthood.

If I were to listen to my Unintelligent Fear, my son would never speak Spanish, would never know my culture or know where his Father comes from. But if I pay attention to my

Intelligent Fear, I would encourage my son and my wife to know my heritage and travel with precaution.

May you consider what are you missing because of your Unintelligent Fear and what are you are about to gain because of your Intelligent Fear. Amen.

Back to Basics: Confession of Belhar

Let me begin with a confession… This is the point where I make such a statement that changes something significant in my life, and in your life, since you are my audience.

Today and for your benefit, we will be concerned about Confessions of the Spirit and not Confessions of Legal nature.

Confessions of the Spirit are those pronunciations with spiritual ramifications, while confessions of legal nature are pronunciations with legal ramifications. Now, sometimes a spiritual confession has legal ramifications, such as the confession of marriage. And sometimes a legal confession (in any of its forms) incurs spiritual ramifications, such as the political death of Jesus Christ on the cross, which brought salvation to all of us.

Now into what is important—spiritual confessions and the spiritual ramifications. You should have guessed by now that I do not have a spiritual confession to make. What I said was more like a statement. But let me keep my promise. I love you because, by the mercy of God, with you I find joy and purpose—that is a big confession. Would you agree?

So, that is a Spiritual Confession, let see if I see any Spiritual Ramifications. Do you see any? Have I changed, or have you have changed? Because you look like the same good-looking people from before, maybe a few seconds older but that is it, I won't tell. So, what is the point of spiritual confessions if nothing happens? Well, there are three things that we must remember about confessions.

Confessions are meaningful, but they are not magical. Confessions are significant but only if they are spoken and received in and with faith. Confessions take us to back to basics, to what is important.

They are meaningful; they are resolutions to an event or circumstance within a community of faith in a precise time and place. But they are not "magical." It does not matter how historical they are, confessions by themselves will not transform you, they will not help you mutate into a holy being, it doesn't matter how much you recite them. But they need to be spoken and received in faith to be able to move mountains and set the record straight.

Church, remember that Faith is for a Christian as oil is for a car; you might cruise for a while, but if you are not paying attention to the oil level or purity, one day you will not make it to where you were planning to go. Now, do not think that you are the car, but the car is where we are all moving.

Faith is not just about you; faith is also about the people who are in this journey of life with you. How you live your faith, or the lack of it, will affect the person next to you. Faith is also about what we share and what we take.

Now, in matters of holiness, confessions are not at the level of scripture, but confessions are important because they point us to scripture and to those who the scriptures are written for.

So right now, we have a few moving pieces, so allow me to recap. Confessions are meaningful but they are not magical. You must speak them and received them in faith. They are about our faith and they point us to Scripture and to whom we need to serve.

But above all confessions take us back to basics. But what is our basic?

Reading now, from the Gospel of Luke 12: 41-48

Peter said, "Lord, are you telling this parable for us or everyone?" 42 And the Lord said, "Who then is the faithful and prudent manager whom his master will put in charge of his slaves, to give them their allowance of food at the proper time? 43 Blessed is that slave whom his master will find at work when he arrives. 44 Truly I tell you, he will put that one in charge of all his possessions. 45 But if that slave says to himself, 'My master is delayed in coming,' and if he begins to beat the other slaves, men, and women, and to eat and drink and get drunk, 46 the master of that slave will come on a day when he does not expect him and at an hour that he does not know, and will cut him in pieces, [a] and put him with the unfaithful. 47 That slave who knew what his master wanted, but did not prepare himself or do what was wanted, will receive a severe beating. 48 But the one who did not know and did what deserved a beating will receive a light beating. From everyone to whom much has been given, much will be required; and from the one to whom much has been entrusted, even more, will be demanded.

Our basic is remembering that we are all under one roof. And yes, I know that we are all under one roof, under 97 E. Genesee St. But I mean generally in the world, we are under one roof. When Peter says, "Lord, are you telling this parable for us (the close disciples but doubting followers) or all?

The question is full of incredibility and perhaps a hint of arrogance that I believe Jesus has no other choice than to say, "Can't you see that you are all slaves?" It doesn't matter what position you have, or what role you play in life; you are servants, retainers, managers, executives, administrators, supervisors—none of us is the owner. but let us stop here— Jesus is not telling us these things to make us feel unimportant or shameful.

Remember that Christ in the gospel of John 15:15 says that

"I do not call you servants any longer because the servant[b] does not know what the master is doing; but I have called you friends because I have made known to you everything that I have heard from my Father."

And so also in Acts 3:25

"You are the descendants of the prophets and of the covenant that God gave to your ancestors, saying to Abraham, 'and in your descendants, all the families of the earth shall be blessed."

Jesus is telling us in Luke 12: 41-48 that we are all slaves, but not to our shame, rather to give us glory. How so? Jesus does not want us to be caught off guard, and for us to be found like the trusted servant in verse 45.

Our basic is remembering that "Everyone to whom much was given, of them much will be required, and from them to whom they entrusted much, they will demand the more." And in here is where confessions play an important role. Take for example the last addition to our Book of Confessions, PCUSA. The Confession of Belhar is a confession that we adopted as a denomination that speaks about many things, especially unity, reconciliation, and justice.

Church, if you have not considered our eleven previous Creed and Confessions, or if you have not even heard about the newest confession—Confession of Belhar—you need to start getting interested in them.

As a congregation, you better start demanding more from your ministers, not in the office, not in the visitation, but in our teachings. After all, we are called Teaching Elders, not administrators, not office managers. You need to know these confessions; they are a significant piece and key elements of our doctrine.

But also, let me give it to you straight. It is also about you wanting to be involved and having the desire to learn and dwell in this confession with us.

These confessions are like answer keys,

- They are full of convictions and actions.
- They guide the church in the study and interpretation of the scriptures.
- They summarize the essence of our Reformed Christian Tradition.
- They direct the Church in maintaining a sound doctrine.
- They equip the congregation for its work of proclamation.
- They help us to witness the life of Jesus Christ in our day and time.

But then now you might be thinking, "Sure Mario," we know you can do the talking, how about the walking. And I must answer you like a Barraquillero; that is a person from the city of Barranquilla. "Si Estoy hablando de tajada, es porque ya la tengo frita." Which translates to something like, if I am talking about fried chicken, that's because it is fried and on the table.

If you see our announcements, you will see that our new and second summer series of adult study and prayer starts on Tuesday at 4:45 pm – my hope is that you take the challenge and study these confessions with me. Now if you cannot come on Tuesday, it is ok. The study is designed to be a take home studies, that you do on your own time, and they have a weekly video available to encourage you and to give you an overview of the week.

To see these videos, you can go to our website, or sign-up to the video email list, and just open them from your email account. Next week, we will have an introduction and finer points of our newest addition to our Book of Confessions, the Confession of Belhar. I hope that you can join us.

May you remember that Confessions are meaningful, but they are not magical. Confessions are significant but only if they are spoken and received in/with faith. Confessions take us to back to basics, to what is important. Amen.

Unity, Reconciliation, and Justice

Last week we talked about how confession and creeds (as they are accepted and include by our denomination) are significant because they are historical, giving us a glimpse of the struggles and challenges. For example, the Confession of Belhar gives us a glimpse of how people in South Africa struggled with a legal degree that forced people to be separated on the ground of race and how the church was a beacon of light.

They are meaningful because they tell us that the church decided to help the efforts of those fighting against the system, thus demonstrating that the church can do more than just talking, even if talking is what they need to be doing. But we realize that this confession is not magical. The Confession of Belhar was written in Belhar, South Africa in 1982 to fight the sin of Apartheid, but the actual abolition of Apartheid didn't take place until 1994 with the democratic general elections.

Confessions need to be spoken of faith, need to be received in faith, and that faith is not an automatic thing, it is not a switch. Some people have an Aha! moment and for others it is a work in progress that takes a lifetime. Finally, these Confessions that we have adopted take us back to the basics, to the cornerstones of our doctrine or in other words, to the bone of the meat, to the seed of the vegetable.

This Confession of Belhar takes us back to consider three things that should be in place before we talk about paying the bill, doing a picnic, having a good feeling sermon, nice music, and comfortable air conditioning. These are Unity, Reconciliation, and Justice.

But before you start thinking that I am about you ask you stand up, and go outside and rally the streets demanding Unity, Reconciliation and Justice, quoting excerpts of the Confession of Belhar, you might need to reconsider. Read Isaiah 5:1-4, in there we read that the farmer did everything right; the ground was fertile, and everything was in place to protect the vineyard. The vineyard was wicked and bore wild grapes!

So, before you go and fix everything that is wrong with the world, we need to remember that often, we are part of the problem. We have to remember that we are wild grapes, good does not come naturally to us. We need to step out of the bubble that we live in and wake-up to our brokenness.

Recognizing our reality will allow us to overcome our reality.

Recognizing our reality will allow us to be intentional in the good deeds that we are called to do. Love doesn't come naturally to us.

Recognizing our reality will allow us to do what we can, when we can, if we can, with what we have, while doing it in the name of Christ Jesus.

Do not glorify yourselves in the good love that you can demonstrate.

Some of you might say. "Those are some harsh things to say, but I guess they make a little bit of sense." Some of you might say... I come to church to feel better and find refuge from the hate of the world and what you are telling me is that I am what is wrong with this world.

But that's not what I am saying. What I am saying to you is a glimpse of what I read in the scriptures. Reading now from the Gospel of Luke 12: 49 – 56

"I came to bring fire to the earth, and how I wish it were already kindled! I have a baptism with which to be baptized, and what stress I am under until it is completed! Do you think that I have come to bring peace to the earth? No, I tell you, but rather division! From now on five in one household will be divided, three against two and two against three; they will be divided: father against son and son against father, mother against daughter and daughter against mother, mother-in-law against her daughter-in-law and a daughter-in-law against mother-in-law." He also said to the crowds, "When you see a cloud rising in the west, you immediately say, 'It is going to rain'; and so, it happens. And when you see the south wind blowing, you say, 'There will be scorching heat', and it happens. You hypocrites! You know how to interpret the appearance of earth and sky, but why do you not know how to interpret the present time?"

Do you know who said that? That was Jesus talking. Jesus was not sarcastic, Jesus was tired, and Jesus was under a lot of stress. Jesus was on his way to Jerusalem; he was on his way to the cross. And between here and there, Jesus was just fed-up with the politics, with the lies, with hate, with the jealousy.

These words are just a few verses away from Jesus teaching us how to pray, Jesus performing miracles, talking about demons, then having a teaching moments with lawyers and church leaders. He was also teaching about being careful with being a hypocrite, the importance of confession before God, the parable of the rich, and how we must not be afraid.

Then he tells us that for the Glory of God, we must remember that we are all equal before the eyes of God; we are children of the covenant, yet we are all slaves. And not one before or above another. And then he gets to the scripture that we just read. I think we have all been there when we are tired and upset and you question if everything that you are doing, and everything that you are yet to do, is worth it.

Now I do not want you to think that Jesus said what he said because he was emotional or tired or had a case of the Mondays. Jesus was unlocking the mystery of our reality as

humans and how we relate to one another. Christ, the anointed one knew what his presence would do to this world.
Christ came to this world to bring peace and unity, but consequently, Christ would also bring division, fights, and the destruction.

I know it sounds like an oxymoron, but this is where knowing the verse, within the chapter, within the book, with the section within the whole scripture comes in handy.

Christ is talking here about the real unity, which happens to be the same unity that the Confession of Belhar is about.

At this point, I wish to remind you that the Confession of Belhar talks or centers its attention on three things: Unity, Reconciliation, and Justice. And because all three of them would make for a very long sermon, I have chosen to speak on behalf of Unity because it is where reconciliation and justice come from.

Unity in Christ does not mean everyone smashes together, looking, talking, thinking, behaving, dreaming and breathing the same thing. Unity in Christ means that we share a vision and that we recognize that we are connected at the basic level. Unity in Christ is so amazing that I cannot put into words how amazing it is. The more I think about it, the more I struggle coming up with an example for it, but here it is.

Friday before last I was playing softball. I was in Fulton, NY. New team, new friends, new fields, new balls, new rules. First inning, two outs, young guy at bat, with a runner on second.

I pitch a curve ball, aiming for the lower corner of the plate. Guy swings makes contact. I see the softball coming. It is no bouncing. It is not going up, thinking to put the glove down, easy snatch, out on first. Third out. Let's go... But what is this pain?

Where is the ball? Can't move that ankle. I am standing, not moving. Don't see the ball only see the guy at the plate with his hands on his head. Umpire is rushing to me. The first baseman, Nate and Chad are rushing to me. Duggy the Catcher is also. The 3rd baseman and the shortstop. Even the outfield is coming to see if I am ok.

I am still standing. I take my facemask off, and look my ankle. I can move it, I can walk, it doesn't hurt. I say, "I am ok guys." Let's play.

For a glimpse, for just a second. That field of softball in Fulton, NY was an example of Unity. Everybody dropped everything else, and the concern was the wellbeing of an outsider, the new guy, in this case me. It didn't matter if the guy at the home plate aimed to hit middle or not. It doesn't matter if it was a team of us versus them. I was hurt, and the world of softball stopped.

Now consider if the world would behave in such away.

Where we know that everybody plays a role and that there are teams looking to win, but not at the expense of someone's pain. Unity is not about us all being on the same team or making sure that we all get equal treatment, or that we all get a trophy at the end of the game. Unity in Christ is about having a vision that goes beyond us. It is about considering everyone equally because that was the vision of Christ.

May you know that unity is more than a concept.

May you remember that everyone is invited to be united in the vision of Christ, but that not everyone will accept the invitation. Don't be discouraged if the people you love dislike Christ's invitation. Exercise grace and love when is possible and rest in the mighty acts of Christ. Amen.

Water. What is it Good for?

Matthew 14: 22 – 33 "Immediately he made the disciples get into the boat and go on ahead to the other side, while he dismissed the crowds. And after he had dismissed the crowds, He went up the mountain by Himself to pray. When evening came, He was there alone, but by this time the boat, battered by the waves, was far from the land, for the wind was against them. And early in the morning, he came walking towards them on the lake. But when the disciples saw him walking on the lake, they were terrified, saying, 'It is a ghost!' And they cried out in fear. But immediately Jesus spoke to them and said, 'Take heart, it is I; do not be afraid.'

Peter answered him, 'Lord if it is you, command me to come to you on the water.' He said, 'Come.' So, Peter got out of the boat, started walking on water, and came towards Jesus. But when he noticed the strong wind, he became frightened, and beginning to sink; he cried out, 'Lord, save me!' Jesus immediately reached out his hand and caught him, saying to him, 'You of little faith, why did you doubt?' When they got into the boat, the wind ceased. And those in the boat worshiped him, saying, 'Truly you are the Son of God.'"

Water can be dangerous, especially if you are misinformed about the benefits of water. Did you know that drinking too much water too quickly can lead to water intoxication which can result in death? Water can be your salvation. Especially if you are informed about the benefits of water.

Did you know that drinking water can/could increase your energy, control your appetitive and help you reduce the risk of certain types of cancers including colon, bladder and breast cancer?

Water is essential either way but did you know that water is of importance to Christians? Water to us is more than the liquid that we drink. It goes beyond that—water has played a major role in our faith journey as it is the creation of God. Water has been a weapon; water has been a shield; water has been a wall; water has been a path; water has been a sign of the covenant; water has medicine; water has been wine; water has been many things for us!

In the Hebraic tradition water isn't just water. Water is the unknown, the place where we cannot easily move, where we cannot breathe air, where things disappear. Water is that relentless liquid that runs and grows with the rain. Indeed, there is something metaphysical about water, something that we cannot fully understand. The idea that we as humans need water to survive, but that water does not need us, is intimidating.

Water was before creation. Water doesn't mind darkness. Water is okay either way. Water exists in darkness and water can exist in light. According to Karl Barth, water, in the first biblical creation story, as "The principle which, in its abundance and power is opposed to God's creation; it is a representative of all the evil forces which oppress and resist the salvation intended for the people of Israel."

Water can be a synonym of disorder or bad things. Examples of that are in Genesis 1:2 "The earth was formless and empty, darkness was over the surface of the deep, and the Spirit of God was hovering over the waters" and then Genesis 1:6 "Let there be a vault between the waters to separate waters from waters." And that it is just to mention a few. But then water can be the synonym of freedom, pureness, and eternal joy. Take, for example, the final deliverance and destruction of Pharaoh's army while parting the Red Sea, and the waters of the Jordan for Baptisms.

Something else to consider, water and a person's life have much in common. A person with her life can save a life or destroy life. A person "like water" can clean, refresh and bring joy to others, but also a person "like water" can kill, destroy a home, and destroy civilizations and bring chaos and sadness. A person "like water" can give freedom or support slavery, but water, unlike us, does not get a choice. Water cannot choose between right and wrong actions. Just remember--Water, drink responsibly! Life, live responsibly!

In life, we have choices just like Peter, and today we will learn from him. From what I have shared with you this morning you can now understand that Jesus isn't just walking on water. Jesus is walking on top of good and bad. Jesus is above everything; He shows a glimpse of his lordship above our fears, above our weapons, above our known and unknown. Jesus Christ by choice shows knowledge that goes beyond all knowledge.

As we recognize that, now I want to pay attention to Peter. Who is Peter in the story? Most people when hearing this story understand a story of faith or lack of it, but this morning I would like to go away from that analysis and perhaps look at other things that might be beneficial to us. Let us talk about Peter, not the mighty disciple, but the ordinary human named "Peter" who is a witness to this event.

The one who makes some radical choices with his life, which might help us with our own.

Of all the things that we can learn from Peter's choices, my top 3 are:

a. If possible, don't bite off more than you can chew.

Which exactly is what Peter is doing in our story. Sometimes in life, we drown by our choices. Often, we are in a good spot during life; everything is not perfect, there are some winds and some waves and you are enduring the unknown of the water. Then like Peter, you decide that you are not going to stay where you are which is your right as a child of the covenant. But then what you end up doing is a bold and unnecessary decision. And what was a manageable, a bit uncomfortable end up being a life-treating situation.

If we look at the scriptures again, you will see that the idea of Peter walking on water was Peter's idea. It wasn't Jesus idea so when Peter starts to drown is nobody but Peter's fault.

I realize that Peter does say "Lord if it is you, command me to come to you on the water." And Jesus says "Come," BUT I mean, what was Jesus supposed to do?

What I believe is happening here is that Jesus is going to use the eagerness of Peter to present an interesting concept. Know your limitations or be ready to face the consequences, whatever they might be! Do not bite off more than you can chew.

b. Before any decision, be in contact with God.

Now in here, Peter makes a comeback. Please realize that Peter before putting a foot out of the boat, makes the assertive decision to get Jesus' attention. After all, Peter had the choice to step out of the boat and swim; Peter is a fisherman, so heavy winds and rough waves are not something new.

So, why was Peter assertive on this? And why does that matter?

Plainly because Peter prayed without knowing. Yes, Peter prayed, and his prayer wasn't the cliché of prayer. Peter was honest with the
Lord with what he wanted. And Jesus replies with an epic word

"COME." Jesus' answer did not include any disclaimers like: well this is water, and you do not have enough faith, or you are

not God so you cannot do this, or even sure, Peter you go and try that if you fail, I will help you and will not let you die.
c. At the end of your story, it will be you and God, and nobody else.

This is another thing that Peter does well in our story. One that speaks of the reality of our relationship with Jesus Christ. Our story begins with Jesus sending all his disciples away in one boat so we can assume that Peter is not alone on this boat. So how come Peter is only attempting to go towards Jesus? Was Peter the only one with the courage to go, or did the other disciples knew their place was on the boat, or was it that Jesus was going towards them so why bother? It might be one of them, all of them or none at all.

What is important is that Peter made a choice to go towards Christ, which is the right choice. Even if you cannot save yourself from drowning, going towards Jesus is always the best choice.

Now, I'm not saying that all of you need to become Ordained Ministers. In fact, there is a quote that summons my thoughts on that subject that says, "If you are happy doing anything else besides ordained ministry, do it."

It doesn't matter what you chose to do in life; you will always go towards Christ in your field of business, vocation or practice. Whether it is Medicine, Engineering, Arts or Music or simply a retiree from office hours or teaching, there is always something that you can do to give glory to God, no matter what.

With Peter, we remember that you might be on a boat, church, house, mission trip, whatever with a bunch of other disciples, friends and/or family. In the end, your walk of faith will be between you and God. Christ knows this, and the expectations are high, and failure is a possibility, but Christ will always be attentive if you chose to go His way.

May we remember on this day the limits of our strength and life, always acting decently and in order, to be prayerful, taking the time to speak and be in contact with God before any action or direction is taken. And always remember that at the end of your days, what you do and do not do in life is between you and God. Amen

What Should We Do to Get Ready?
"Live Honorably as in the day."

The writer of the letter to the Ephesians gives us several pieces of advice or recommendations on how to protect us against some of the things that life might toss our way.

I say they are recommendations because, in all honesty, nobody is going to be policing you into making sure to follow these recommendations, these are not the commandments. It is not like when you are driving on Genesee St, and you see the 30mph Speed Limit white sign—that it is not a recommendation— that is a law, and we have police officers whose job it is to enforce such a law.

What we see in the letter to the Ephesians are recommendations—just like the many recommendations that you receive from friends, coaches or loving significant others. But these recommendations are inspired by the Holy Spirit.

Church, God here is telling you to make sure you are wearing your helmet—doesn't matter if you are just learning how to ride the bike or you have won the Tour de France, it's just silly—If not something else—to not use one if someone already paid the price for it.

I remember when I started to play softball and I started to pitch; a good friend of mine name Reese told me that as I started to play competitive softball I would need a facemask. I remember laughing out loud, and telling him that I had a glove so I wouldn't need a facemask. He said "ok, pretty face." At the end of our game, he gave me his facemask and told me to try it.

Not even 48 hours later while playing in a qualifying tournament in a state championship, I got smacked so hard by a softball that the facemask that Reese gave me broke. That was six years ago, and since then I have gone from plastic to metal.

Now, in life, a helmet only covers a portion of your body, a significant part of it, but still just a part. Wouldn't it be better to have whole body armor? And even then, an armor only increases your chances of surviving in life; they cannot guarantee that the impacts or hits in life will be painless or that nothing bad will happen to you while you are alive.

The purpose of armor is to make you able to stand against the tricks and wiles of the accuser or deceiver. The purpose of the armor is you help you, not to save you, because the one that paid for your helmet is the only one that by Grace saves you.

Some of you might know that not only am I preaching today—glory be to God—but also, I have the wonderful opportunity, the blessing and the privilege of preaching next Sunday.

And so, God has put in my heart by the Holy Spirit a short series on "What should we do to get ready?" And "What should we do once we are ready?"

What should we do to get ready? Please join me as I read our second scripture for this morning found in Roman 13: 11-14

"Besides this, you know what time it is, how it is now the moment for you to wake from sleep. Salvation is nearer to us now than when we became believers; the night is far gone; the day is near. Let us then lay aside the works of darkness and put on the armor of light; let us live honorably as in the day, not in reveling and drunkenness, not in debauchery and licentiousness, not in quarreling and jealousy. Instead, put on the Lord Jesus Christ, and make no provision for the flesh, to gratify its desires."

The first thing that we need to do, Church is to wake up, says the scriptures. You know what time it is, how the moment is now for you to wake from sleep.
How important it is to awake out of sleep! We can do many Christian things "To have Christian-like behavior" and essentially be asleep towards God.

Church, we need to wake-up: the things that we do, we do on behalf of God for the love of God's people. But what God wants from us is the "US" not what we "DO!"

Do you see the difference? And how important that difference is? Just like your spouse is happy with the flowers that you bought her, or that you are happy with the colorful bowtie that she bought for you. The thing that we want is not a thing; what we want is a meaningful, everlasting and significant relationship with the person on the other side of the gift.

Church, we need to wake-up because the world is full of Christians who are doing amazing things, but are half asleep not knowing that today we are close to the glorious return of our Lord Jesus Christ. Today we are closer than yesterday and tomorrow we will closer than today!

The second thing that we need to do, Church, is to pick up that armor of light that God gave us and wear it every day. There are too many people out there living their lives without that armor.

For spiritual safety, you need to help each other and check the straps, the clips and make sure it fits tight and is well maintained.

When you get dressed every day, you dress appropriately to who you are and what you plan to do. Therefore, every day make sure that you are checking with the maker of your armor. Call that 1-800 number.

Daily, request the creator and maker of that armor to make it stronger and adaptable. Make sure you are keeping up with all the updates and request new functions as you are facing different challenges from a year ago.

You are doing yourself a disfavor if you think that the armor that you had five years ago, or even last year or last Sunday is still working for you with all the new challenges that you are facing right now.

Today is your opportunity to reflect on how you are protecting yourself. Just as you are keeping an eye on your clothes for work, or what improvement can be made on your looks or physique, you need to pray and request for God to improve your spiritual armor.

Finally, the third thing that you need to do, Church, is to be able to identify those things that are drawing the light out of you.

It will be easy and comfortable to tell you about the meaning of these words (that we find in verse 13 and 14) and then tell you to walk away from them or stop doing them and then consider my work done.

But I want to be helpful and not pretend to be righteous before you.

I am going to tell you the list before us, and then I am going to tell you what my recommendation as your pastor is.

The words are Reveling that speaks about the abuse of partying too much or being lost in the socializing world. Drunkenness that speaks on a state of permanent intoxication or impairment, where you are no longer you. Debauchery that speaks about a state of corruption and dishonesty.

Licentiousness that speaks about a state of desire for a forbidden bed; a person who holds no sexual fidelity. Quarreling that speaks about a state of perpetual fighting arguing and disagreeing personality. Jealousy that speaks about a permanent state of suspicion, distrust, and possessiveness.

That's a list of things or actions that, if you can avoid, you will be a better and more faithful Christian which should be the goal of every Christian in this sanctuary. But staying away from doing and behaving is such away is no differently than what the young ruler was doing before he found Jesus and was challenged to sell all his possessions.

And so, I want to make my recommendation; I will like to direct your attention to Romans 13: 13a, to the words that say "Live honorably as in the day."

Those are words that preach themselves and what I want you to do, is to add those six words to your daily prayer. Pray as you normally pray, and in your prayer, ask God to help you to "live honorably as in the day."

Allow God to touch you in prayer, allow God to guide you through that list of things to avoid and show you true potential as a child of God.

May you remember to be ready by waking up and giving priority to the relationship that God wants with you! May you remember to be ready by picking up and never taking off if possible the Armor of God! May you remember to be ready by asking God to help you "Live Honorably as in the day." Amen.

What Should We Do Once We Are Ready?
"The Armor of God"

Last week we talked about the power of our armor of light, and how important is to keep it updated and in good shape. We do it by seeking the counsel of God by way of prayer, the study of scripture and Christian community discernment. We talk about how the armor is not intended to help you avoid the attacks, rather it helps to prevent fatal blows. We talked about how wearing that armor of light was a recommendation and not something God is going to make you do.

Also, we learned last week from reading Romans 13: 11-14 that there are at least three things that as a Christian you should do to be ready.

- To wake up from how busy we are and pay attention to the relationship that we have with God.
- To make sure that you were using the Armor of light that was provided to you by the sacrifice of Jesus Christ.
- To avoid a few behaviors that were sucking the light out of your armor, such as drunkenness, debauchery, and jealousy.

But today is a new day with a new lesson; I have been called to give you another boost, to energize you, to give you confidence. I am not a coach; I am a field player just like you. Our coach is Jesus Christ and He is waiting for us at the field.

Read Ephesians 6: 10 -18

We just heard about being strong, about the whole armor, about who's your enemy and what the enemy is trying to do with you. It tells you about the belt of truth around your waist and is all about the breastplate of righteousness. And you know at this point, it might sound like God is telling you to cover yourself with this heavy stuff, all this metal, but you need to stop thinking like that. Let me tell you why! Around verse 15, it says, "shoes for your feet put on whatever will make you ready to proclaim the gospel of peace" Does that sound like something heavy and limiting to you?

To me that means that you have freedom. God is telling you— I like who you are, I like your ideas, I like your thoughts, in fact, I want you to use what I am giving you, but I also want you to use those things that make you special. God likes you. Did you know that in fact, God loves you—did you know that?! Especially when you are using what God gave you for the benefit of others, but that's not all. In verse 16 says to take the shield and then verse 17 talks about the helmet which we talked about last week. But then it says to take the sword.

Wait! This isn't looking like armor anymore. There is something else going on here. God is not giving you armor so you can make it shine and make it look pretty. He is not giving the best of the best so you can lock yourself between the walls of the church and look fancy.

That's like getting a new Ford F-150 Platinum and never taking it outside of the dealership where it was given to you. I mean it might last forever, but I am sure that is not the purpose for it. Right? And so, that's where we begin. Allow me the pleasure to read our second lesson, found in the book of James 1:2-6:

"My brothers and sisters, [a] whenever you face trials of any kind, consider it nothing but joy, three because you know that the testing of your faith produces endurance; 4 and let endurance have its full effect, so that you may be mature and complete, lacking in nothing. 5 If any of you is lacking in wisdom, ask God, who gives to all generously and ungrudgingly, and it will be given you. 6 But ask in faith, never doubting, for the one who doubts is like a wave of the sea, driven and tossed by the wind."

Church, on this day of worship, as we meet inside these walls, we need to acknowledge that God didn't want you to stay here with your faith. Instead, God wanted us to run free with that faith! Let me propose a few things that might be helpful to you as you move forward.

Make a choice and pick the right shoe. In the awareness that God is generous, make sure that you are using what God already gave you! God wants you to be involved; God doesn't want you to disappear and make you his puppet. God is allowing you to put in your two-cents and sometimes much more! But what if you don't know what pair of shoes is the best? What if you have way too many choices and only two feet? What if you don't even know what shoes look like?

Our second scripture of this morning is telling us that if any of you, myself included, are lacking in wisdom, we need to ask God, who gives to all generously and ungrudgingly, that we would be without envy or reluctance.

By now, you should know that for our lesson, shoes equal aptitudes or talents. In James verse 5 we read that if you lack the wisdom to choose what aptitude or talents you should use, you should ask God to help you pick—just like you would ask your spouse what type of shoes you should wear. Know that the appeal here is not to request a talent, but to choose one of the many that you already have.

Walk with confidence, with the Effective Shield. Now you might be asking, if God gave you an armor to protect you, why is God also giving you a shield? I believe the answer starts with something like, it's not only about you!

Imagine that you are going down the street, and you have all your armor, you are protected, and you also have your shield with you. Then next to you, there is a person walking. You love this person very much. In fact, this person is your parent.

You two are walking, and out of nowhere there is a flaming arrow, like the ones that the letter to the Ephesians was describing. But you are okay because you have your armor and you know that the arrow won't do much damage. But then you realize that your parent who is next to you doesn't have on his armor. Well, then you use your shield to protect your parent next to you, not only yourself.

It sounds like a good story, but let us make it real. Imagine that you are at the office and you have a coworker next to you. You are both good workers, and one difference between you and your coworker is that you know you are worthy of love because you know Christ died for you.

Your coworker is in a rough relationship and your coworker is being bullied by their significant other. Your coworker has low self-esteem. What do you do? You need to use your shield and make sure that your coworker knows that it doesn't matter what the other person says or believes. We are all worthy of love, compassion, and understanding. Now, you are using your shield in an effective way.

Now, the one thing that you always need to keep in mind is that at the time of using the effective shield you need to do it in faith without doubt while asking God to direct your movements, your words, and actions. James verse 6 says "The one who doubts is like a wave of the sea, driven and tossed by the wind." Church let us do everything with faith, in decency and order—the worst thing is to get hurt by trying to help someone because then both of you might need help.

God has given you tools to be used. God is letting you pick your comfortable shoes or talents. God is giving you a Shield for your "safeguard and the safety of those around you" But now God is giving you a sword to make sure the world knows that God means business.

Weapons are no joke. Sure, you can use them for protection, but what if you don't know how to use it? I wonder what your thoughts are on sword control. Sword control? Yes. Or in other words, Bible control.

Ephesians say, "The sword of the Spirit is the word of God." Such an idea is not only found in Ephesians but is also found in the letter to Hebrew 4: 12 "For the word of God is living and active, sharper than any two-edged sword, piercing to the division of soul and of spirit, of joints and marrow, and discerning the thoughts and intentions of the heart."

Bible control? Well, sometimes people like to quote the bible, perhaps too much. Have you ever heard the words "The devil can cite Scripture for his purpose?" Do these words make sense? Yes. Are these words true? Yes. Are these words in the Bible? No.

In Genesis 3 and Matthew 4, you read about the devil quoting scripture. The issue in not the quoting of the Bible, or using the sword. It's misquoting the Bible and misusing the sword. The scriptures are there; they are not going anywhere. It's up to you to be informed. It's interesting to note, just because someone quotes scripture doesn't mean they're imparting the truth correctly. Like the devil, some people can use the bible for their purpose. The Bible is power; it is a weapon, a sword with two edges that can destroy your enemy, or can destroy you. But you are not the Bible you have a choice!

Most deceitful uses of scripture can be exposed by reading the context of the text, by analyzing scripture within scripture, and by being mindful of the salvific acts of Jesus on the Cross.

Church you need to know your Bible; it is not so you can quote it, rather it is so that you are not fooled or attacked by your own sword. Church, I believe that every Christian has everything they need to make the difference around themselves. We need to remember that God grants us time and allow us to get ready, but then God expects us to go out there.

What we do in church on Sunday morning is to give glory to God and regroup so we can continue until God calls us to God's kingdom.

May you remember to wake up from being busy and make sure you are wearing the armor of light. Always ask God to help you avoid the dark behavior that drains the light out of you. May you remember that God is not a master puppet. God wants you to bring your talents and your gifts to the table. Remember the shield for your safety and make sure you know that there is power the behind your sword. Amen

Are You a Procrastinator?

A procrastinator is a person who delays or puts things off. Have you been called a procrastinator? Church, don't worry; I'm not going to ask you to raise your hand, but I do want to make things personal. So, church you need to ask me… "Have you been called a procrastinator?" The answer is yes, in both English and Spanish.

The good news is that sometimes I do it on purpose, like when I am preparing a class, making a video or writing a sermon. I will stop what I am doing to visit someone, read a page of something entirely off topic, or visit other churches' websites, or more recently this morning when I was pouring the water into our baptism font.

In the beginning, I started doing it because I was troubled that the lesson, sermon or video would just become a task to accomplish. Just something to check off the list. But then something started to happen; the more I would "Lose" control, the more I felt God gaining control. The less of me, allowed more of God. And then I started to realize that this idea of procrastinating has amazing spiritual ramifications.

Now I do have you give you a disclaimer.

I am not telling you to procrastinate at your job, or with your duties in your household, or with your homework is a good idea. Remember that God is glorified when we act with decency and in order.

What I am saying is that we have overcorrected ourselves and we have started to worship the Father time, Clock the son and the Holy Calendar, and we have pushed our faith aside and have left God on the sidelines. Time is nothing, yet we worship time. We are always making sure that we are on time and that we accomplish a task promptly. We value time as the biggest commodity.

You know what God says about time? 2 Peter 3: 8 – 9

"but do not ignore this one fact, beloved, that with the Lord one day is like a thousand years, and a thousand years are like one day. 9 The Lord is not slow about his promise, as some think of slowness, but is patient with you, not wanting any to perish, but all to come to repentance. But the day of the Lord will come like a thief, and then the heavens will pass away with a loud noise, and the elements will be dissolved with fire, and the earth and everything that is done on it will be disclosed."

Today Church I do not want to challenge you, I do not want to give you homework, or another thing to be added to that already overbooked, overscheduled, overstretched agenda of yours. Can we just relax?

Church, it would do you good to procrastinate, but not just any procrastinating that would-be laziness. Want I want you to do is to add procrastinating to your agenda, procrastinate with a purpose, and procrastinate in the name of God.

Church, starting today. I want you to find the time to stop, collaborate and listen to the voice of God in the midst and the rush of this world. To put things into perspective, look at the story as is found in Genesis, the story of creation. So, as we know it, the story of creation took a few days.

Every day God created something. But why? God being who God is, and having the power that God has, why did God consider taking it slow, and procrastinate when God could have built everything with a snap of God's fingers? I believe was because God knew the importance of not rushing, and how only those who know how to rest, know how to work.

Now, I am not saying that you should become a procrastinator, what I am saying is that everyone is somehow a procrastinator and that if we do it in the name of God, your quality of life will improve your creativity and vision for your life. You will get a better vantage point, your stress levels will be forced to go down, and your will have a healthier memory.

If you go around life pretending that you keep up with Father time, you will crash into the stress of more. Remember that when you rush, you become average. Remember that the turtle wins at the end. Not because it was smarter or faster, but because the turtle was true to her nature. Would you be true to your nature? Would you slow down and take Sabbath?

Do what you can when you can but don't try to do everything. May you by slowing down feel power of God, and be release from the chains of schedule. Amen.

Serve One Another

Last week we started to talk about two things, miracles and servitude. We talked about how we need to be intentional with our feelings and desires when we pray for God to perform a miracle. We talked about how our prayers for miracles cannot only be about us and about what we want, but also, they cannot only be about what the friend or loved one wants. Our prayers for miracles need to be about what God wants for us. Today I want to focus on servitude, and for that, I want to read and examine the same scripture that we read last Sunday, but focus on different verses.

Reading again, Gospel of Luke 17:5-10

"The apostles said to the Lord, 'Increase our faith!' The Lord replied, 'If you had faith the size of a mustard seed, you could say to this mulberry tree, 'Be uprooted and planted in the sea,' and it would obey you. Who among you would say to your slave who has just come in from plowing or tending sheep in the field, 'Come here at once and take your place at the table'? Would you not rather say to him, 'Prepare supper for me, put on your apron and serve me while I eat and drink; later you may eat and drink'? Do you thank the slave for doing what was commanded? So, you also, when you have done all that you were ordered to do, say, 'We are worthless slaves; we have done only what we ought to have done!'"

Now, having read that perhaps you might be thinking. How do you go from miracles to servitude? How are miracles and servitude linked? Miracles and servitude are linked by transformation. But what does that even mean?

What are miracles if not the transformation of a person's current reality into a different reality by the grace of God and with the purpose of glorifying God's name? Well, the same applies to servitude.

What is servitude if not the transformation of a person's motivation into a different motivation by the grace of God and with the purpose of glorifying God's name? I think most of you would agree with the first statement, the one about miracles, but I think you would not as easily agree with my second statement, the one regarding servitude.

Most of us would link servitude with slavery, abuse, and oppression, but in Christ and by Christ, servitude is different. But where does this idea of transformation come from? It comes from the faith we profess. It comes from the stuff that miracles are made of. It comes from actions with the intention of giving the glory and exalting God's name above all.

If not, why do you think Jesus, in the beginning, was God and was with God, and became flesh? Well, that shows right there a miracle, and why Jesus was made into flesh to serve the father, which we call a transformation.

A transformation that was made perfect in the transfiguration of our Lord. Remember that Transfiguration does not mean the same thing as Transformation. Transformation implies a remaking of the nature of a person or object. Transfiguration implies a revelation of the true nature. Remember that the beginning of transfiguration is transformation, but if the whole thing still tastes like diet coke mixed with milk, let me present it to you in a different way.

In Luke 17:7 Jesus is asking us that if we had a servant, how many of us would invite them to join you at the table, and not only that, but would have reserved spot at the table after a day of work? Now, when Jesus says that. Is Jesus asking you what you would do, or is Jesus talking about what He is doing with you and me?

If you read, Luke 17:8, you realize that Jesus knows not our response to the question, but what our sinful nature would make us do: Giving more work to the servants and making them wait while we take care of ourselves.

But Mario we do not have servants. And I say, are you sure? Don't fool yourself; you might not call them servants or slaves, but someone is always working like a slave for someone else. In the same way, some of you are diligent, compassionate and help the poor, the widows and the orphans and all those who can be easily our servants. Some of you are doing Christ's work.

Then in Luke 17:9 it says, "Do you thank the slave for doing what was commanded?" Wait; did Jesus just call you His slave? I think He did. I think Jesus is asking you. Should I honor and praise you for your doing what I told you to do? If you are just doing good, coming to church on Sunday, looking at the clock when we have gone over the 60 minutes, putting money in the offering plate sometimes because it is the good Christian thing to do, then you are worthless slaves who are only doing what you were to do.

Church, that is not just some idea. That is what it says on Luke 17:10. "So YOU also, when YOU have done all that YOU were ordered to do, say, 'WE are worthless slaves; We have done only what we ought to have done!" Jesus calls us "slaves" because we are to follow his steps Matthew 20:28 "Just as the

Son of Man Came not to be served but to serve, and to give his life a ransom for many."

Our challenge today is for us to be transformed. Be transformed and let yourself be happy serving. Don't look at the identity of the servant as a low identity, instead cloth yourself with the servant leadership identity. Say to one another today "I will serve you, and I will do it with joy. I will lay my life if necessary for your well-being knowing that the charge is to serve one another, just like Jesus did."

Church, I believe we have the capacity to exceed the expectation of God, but we cannot do it by ourselves. Think about it like this, if I am your servant, and you are my servant, then we will be allowed to call together in unison. Nobody is Lord, except Jesus Christ our Lord.

May you remember that everything begins by accepting the Faith that we already have. May we remember to pray for things considering first the Glory of God. May we remember to serve one another, doing what is required of us, and to pray to God to grant us the wisdom to go beyond God's expectations. Amen.

The Illness of Vanity

In our Bible study on Wednesdays, we are currently reading the book of 1 Samuel. We just finished chapter 16 where Samuel was in charge to anoint a new ruler for Israel. We are in the midst of the transition between Saul and David.

Reading now 1 Samuel 16: 7 "But the Lord said to Samuel, "do not look on his appearance or the height of his stature because I have rejected him. For the Lord sees not as man sees: man looks on the outward appearance, but the Lord looks on the heart." This verse is one of many verses where the evil of vanity, of being prideful and thinking too much of oneself is addressed.

But why is vanity an evil, and why should we try to be like the Lord and look at what is inside rather than our outward appearance? Vanity I will say. The issue of vanity is as old as Adam and Eve. In fact, wasn't vanity the root of the problem?

Everybody can be a victim and suffer from the illness of vanity; particularly this illness affects those who are in charge or are leaders. You will see it at school when a student has a crush on the teacher. You will see it at work when the manager bullies the new employee. And you will see it especially at Church when the leader takes advantage of the position to steal, punish, judge, gossip, and God knows what else.

It doesn't matter what setting you are in; there is always an issue between the personal interest of leaders versus the interest and needs of the community of followers.

Let us now read Mark 10: 35-45

The paradox between vision and vanity is huge. To put things into context, Jesus just shares the news of his judgment, humiliation, and suffering. In response, His disciples are thinking about fame and glory. Word by word, Jesus says, "you do not know what you are asking!"

They do understand the implications of drinking from the same cup and being baptized with the same baptism. Let me remind you about Matthew 26:39 where Jesus prays "my father, if it is possible, let this cup pass from me; yet not as I will, but as you will." Church, we are no different than these disciples. We are not paying attention, and we have the world full of consequences out there for us. The hope is that we have a God that is always paying attention, especially when we don't. We ought to remember what I said earlier; everybody suffers from the illness of vanity, just like everybody is a sinner. Nobody is exempt from experiencing vanity, and it doesn't matter what setting you are in.

The word "giving" is a huge and appropriate environment for the illness of vanity to grow. Notice that I said the word, "giving," and not the act of giving. The word "giving" comes from the brain that being the three pounds of the convoluted mass of gray and white matter in our heads serving to control and coordinate mental and physical actions. The act of giving comes from here heart and mind—In both testament the word "heart" is used to refer to the whole of the innermost part of the human—now I have no way to prove this argument, but tell me if it doesn't feel right, would you follow your mind and heart rather than your brain??

Using the "heart and mind" to do something is better than the "brain" alone. The act of giving should come from the place were God abides, "heart and mind," and not from the place that people control, the "brain." You feel the difference between both of them?

Now, do not hear me saying that a good and faithful "giving" (like God intended) cannot come from using the "brain" and the "heart and mind" what I am saying is that the "giving" that please the Lord cannot come from the "brain" alone.

Again, the word "giving" comes from the "brain" and it is a huge and appropriate environment for the illness of vanity to grow. When we give from the "brain," we start thinking that it is about us. We are the owners; we are giving—because of our power to give. When I give what belongs to me, people should be thankful.

Vanity is an illness, and there is a treatment, but there is no cure. You cannot fix it; you cannot get rid of it. Vanity is a sin and like the sin that it is, the treatment is God. I would consider two treatments that would help us to improve.

One—know, affirm and witness who God is.

Read Job 38: 1-7

Let us consider our first scripture verses 2, 4 and 5. There you will see three major questions, which are the beginning of our treatment. The first question is found in verse 2 "Who are you?" The second question is found in verse 4 "Where were you?" The third question is found in verse 5 "What do you know?"

These questions in the life and testimony of the Christian faith put things into perspective for us. Through them our priorities are corrected and we can begin the treatment process.

In our answer, we shall discover that: God is the one who knows our identity. God is the one that knows our place. And God is the one that has all knowledge.

By knowing, affirming and witnessing God, we see our place as children of God. We acknowledge that we are not giving of what belongs to us, rather we are returning from what we have received.

Two—servant leadership

Going back to the gospel of Mark, we see that after the disciples' demand. Jesus is forced to challenge the world's views on servitude.

It is the old "going to ask you a favor and you can't say no!", demand.

Christ knows that the world believes that being a servant is about following orders, about being poor of spirit, and having a low social status. And leadership is equal to power, glamor, material acquisitions, prestige over people or community. Christ knows that the world believes this, and He is against it.

God's way of leadership is through Servant Leadership. But what is Servant Leadership? Well if you are not serving one another you are not leaders in the eyes of God. If you are serving yourself, you might be a leader within the views of this world, but you will never be a leader before the eyes of God. If we claim to be leaders, we must fight the urgency to put ourselves first. The church and its congregation need to be careful, and we need to consider our motives before acting or before any project. We can be servant leaders when caring for one another is more important than doing things our way. When ministering and serving one another becomes our priority, we will grow to a spiritual level that we have never experienced before, and the miracles of God will be clear for us.

Giving because of vanity is a sin, and assuming that the only thing that we should offer to God is money is also an issue of vanity. If throughout the sermon you were thinking that I was only talking about money (about giving) you have something to double check within yourself. Our wealth and money is something that we should offer to God, but it shouldn't the only thing that you offer to God. You should offer everything that was given to you by God's grace.

May God help us to understand our brokenness as we experience vanity in our church and our families and communities! May God support us as we are challenged by the Bible to know God, to affirm God's dominion over all, and acknowledging God's infinite understanding. May we remember by God's grace to serve one another as God served us first. Amen

Talk about Giving

Last Sunday we talked about the importance of the act of giving. We talked about how the act of giving needs to come from the "Mind and Soul" and not from the "Brain." A giving that comes from the "Brain" is the giving that you do from your leftovers, and in reality, if you give from your leftovers you are better off not giving anything. Giving from our leftovers feeds the illness of vanity within us, it makes us feel like we accomplish something, and we are generous. But God does not want your leftovers; God wants the first fruits, says Proverbs 3:9

We also talked about how "the illness of vanity" is what makes this world believe that when we are in worship, and the minister talks about giving, the minister is out to get your money. We all know the stories, in fact, some people say that's why they do not go to church—because the pastors steal the money.

Now that sometimes is true but most times is a cop-out. So, let me put something out there, right now. Today, I will be talking about giving, and I will not be talking about money. I will be talking about something far more precious than money.

Can you guess what it is? What is the one thing most people say on the deathbed, they wish they had more? Four Letter word that starts with "T." Your Associate Pastor will be talking about TIME!

If you pay attention to the end of the Book of Job, you will read that the Lord restored the fortunes of Job after he had prayed for his friends (being thankful allows you to put things into perspective) and "the Lord gave Job twice as much as he had before." Job 42: 10b

We read about how Job got money and gold from his brothers and sisters, how he got the biggest petting zoo, a coed softball team and that his daughters were prettier than Jennie Finch. But you know the best comes at the end. Job lived to see all of his children and his grandchildren for four generations. And Job had the blessing of dying old and full of days.

But like I said, that is the end of the story, but we need to go back. We need to go back to learn about how Job got to experience the ending that we just read.

Reading now from Job 42: 1-6 "I know that you can do all things and that no purpose of yours can be thwarted. Who is this that hides counsel without knowledge?' Therefore, I have uttered what I did not understand, things too wonderful for me, which I did not know. 'Hear, and I will speak; I will question you, and you declare to me.' I had heard of you by the hearing of the ear, but now my eye sees you; therefore, I despise myself, and repent in dust and ashes."

Personally, I consider this verse to be the crucial part of the book. This is the part of the story when Job can visualize the horizon, and how he was able to move forward after taking such a beating. Here is when the music changes and you see that the good guy is going to the come up on top. This is when the story gives you goose bumps and people get the urge to start clapping.

Job is before God and he makes the following statement of Faith.

a. Nothing happens without God's consent. Job 42: 2
b. At some point, everything will become clear. Job 42: 3-4
c. Allow me to know you; not just have some knowledge of you. Job 42: 5

Now as Christians that is something that we need to keep in mind, and make a mental note and remember as much as we can (especially when we struggle). This knowledge needs to be engraved in our hearts and minds.

Why? Well, it's knowledge about the principality of God, and a reality check for us. As citizens of this great nation, we believe in happy endings, and God is telling us that a happy ending is possible only if it brings Glory to God's name.

With God, everything is about timing, and that includes learning. We need to learn about Job's discovery when life is good and you are above water. Because when you are drowning you are not going to have the time to learn anything, you will only have time to react and I hope that your reaction is to go towards God and not away from God.

Job's statement of faith teaches us that with God, things are on God's time and God's knowledge, not about what we want or what is convenient to us. God does not follow human's expectation.

Job 42:11 says, "They showed him sympathy and comforted him for all the evil that the Lord had brought upon him." It is not an easy to swallow that God allows bad things to happen. But there is a plan, and the plan is for us to help each other to deal with the bad stuff.

But if the plan is for us to help each other, why do we need God? Well, because God is the one that gives you the talents, the opportunity, the life, the purpose and the reward for doing so. We need each other for no other reason. That was the intent from the beginning.

Personally, the purpose of the book of Job for me is to tell us that we are never alone, even if you feel alone. The story teaches us that we are meant to comfort each other and that nobody, especially innocent people, is never meant to be alone while suffering. I could attempt to explain why bad things happen, but the only thing that I would be accomplishing is minimizing the pain and suffering of those who are experiencing those bad things or their suffering.

Our duty is to care for people. We are in the business of loving people, not in the business of offering apologies on behalf of God or offering explanations as to why God allows bad things to happen.

Never try to explain why people suffer, never say God has a plan, never say God closes a door but opens a window. Never say things like "God needed another angel in heaven," and especially never say "God never gives you more than you can handle." They are not helpful. You say those things because the pain of another human being makes you unconformable.

Church, God has called you to comfort each other by being there, not by attempting to explain why things happen; that is God's duty. With that in mind, our purpose is to help each other. Amen.

Christ the King

Did you know that today is a special day in the life of the church? Today we celebrate one the most underappreciated celebrations of our liturgical calendar which is Christ the King Sunday!

It might not be as popular as the events that we celebrate in Advent (which begins next Sunday), but it is still very important to our faith and system of beliefs.

You would think that this celebration started with Christianity itself, I mean Christ is King. Seems pretty obvious to me that the early church would say and proclaim something like that but in fact, this tradition started probably about 80 plus years ago.

It was proclaimed by Pope Pius XI in the year 1925 which was a time of tension. Struggles of war, famine, and depression were everywhere. There were lots of people seeking for a truth and a lot of people proclaiming that they knew and understood the Truth.

The world was watching, waiting for answers, and listening to powerful men competing for the limelight, and the Pope felt that it was time to call on Christian people everywhere to declare their allegiance to the rule of Christ.

Unfortunately, we know how the story plays out. We can say with some certainty that not enough people took Pius' call to Christ seriously, and a lot of people started to pay attention to guys like Mussolini and Hitler.

It is easy to look back and shake our heads, point fingers and judge the leaders of back then, but look at what is happening to our leaders of now? It looks like we have learned nothing, and that we are bound to repeat and let our leaders repeat the mistakes from 90 years ago.

I pray to God for history not to repeat itself, and for us to understand our role in addressing the issues of our world. To speak frankly, I want God to continue to change this world, and I want God to begin with me.

I know that most of you have heard the quote from Eldridge Cleaver that says, "You are either part of the problem or part of the solution". I am here to tell you that it is not a matter of either-or, it is a matter of knowing that you are both; one that is natural to us, and the other that is the path to the cross.

Let us read our second scripture of the day, found in John 18: 33 – 37,

"Then Pilate entered the headquarters[a] again, summoned Jesus, and asked him, "Are you the King of the Jews?" 34 Jesus answered, "Do you ask this on your own, or did others tell you about me?" 35 Pilate replied, "I am not a Jew, am I? Your nation and the chief priests have handed you over to me. What have you done?" 36 Jesus answered, "My kingdom is not from this world. If my kingdom were from this world, my followers would be fighting to keep me from being handed over to the Jews. But as it is, my kingdom is not from here." 37 Pilate asked him, "So you are a king?" Jesus answered, "You say that I am a king. For this, I was born, and for this I came into the world, to testify to the truth. Everyone who belongs to the truth listens to my voice."

This is a familiar text that is usually preached about on this "Jesus the King Sunday", and it is a text that exposes the eschatological truth of Jesus of Nazareth as King. In Layman terms, this is how the story ends, with Christ being the King.

You and I are not familiar with the Office Kingship; that's a concept that is out of our reality. We might know what that means, yet none of us can say that we know what it feels like.

And because kingship is such a strange concept to us, I would like for us to challenge the text and ourselves and exchange the word "King" for "Truth".

Then Pilate entered the headquarters again, summoned Jesus, and asked him, "Are you the truth of the Jews?" 34 Jesus answered, "Do you ask this on your own, or did others tell you about me?" 35 Pilate replied, "I am not a Jew, am I? Your nation and the chief priests have handed you over to me. What have you done?" 36 Jesus answered, "My truthfulness is not from this world. If my truthfulness were from this world, my followers would be fighting to keep me from being handed over to the Jews. But as it is, my truthfulness is not from here." 37 Pilate asked him, "So you are the truth?" Jesus answered, "You say that I am the truth. For this, I was born, and for this I came into the world, to testify to about the Kingdom. Everyone who belongs to the kingdom listens to my voice."38 Pilate asked him, "What is the kingdom?"

Now, I did this as an exercise in my study of the text; we are often encouraged to read a text in preparation for a sermon and to read it multiple times from different bibles and different languages, if possible, and pray and read, and the pray again.

The idea is to allow the text and your senses to dwell in each other and to see if there is something that you have not seen before. This should be done when the text that you are reading is a familiar text.

From this exercise, I saw that Jesus never really treasured or desired the office of kingship, that was something that Pilate brought up, not Jesus.

The whole idea of kingship and God is nice and all but God is eternal, and the office or identity of King is limiting—after all kingdoms fall and kings are replaced, yet the truth of Christ never dies, and it cannot be fully replaced.

See at one point in the beginning of verse 37, Jesus is astute with Pilate, and then Jesus drops the whole act about being king and all. And then it seems that what Jesus is talking about is about He being the truth.

Jesus is talking about being the truth from the get-go; which goes nicely with the whole Gospel according to John that is different in vocabulary. John does not portray Jesus talking much at all about the "kingdom of God [heaven]" as the Synoptics do.

We don't hear story parables from Jesus' mouth. John is filled with an entirely different vocabulary: light and darkness, life, truth, witness, abide, the world, believe, Father and Son, Jesus' "hour," glory, etc.

Furthermore, John shows no secret about Jesus' identity. Jesus is acknowledged with Messianic titles six times in the first chapter alone.

The turning point in the Synoptic Gospels is Peter's confession that Jesus is the Messiah, halfway through the story. Up until that point, the gospels, especially the Gospel according to Mark emphasize a season in which there was a "Messianic Secret," when Jesus forbade the disciples to go public.

Jesus being the truth makes sense, but what does that mean to us? Especially to us now, in a time such as this, when the reality is subjective, and people love to say, "Truth is in the eye of the beholder."

Of all things, my top 3 things to consider are:

1 - Get unstuck; walk away from how you box God and the structure and barriers that you have created for God. We ought to stop assuming that we are in control and embrace the reality that is in front of us.

2 - Build from your reality and avoid dwelling on the expectation of how things should be.

3 - Avoid arrogance; struggling with your faith is acceptable, questioning your faith is essential, asking questions and expecting answers are normal but judging God is reproachable.

Do not begin a conversation from a place of power. Welcome the journey and the struggle with those who disagree with you, and worship with them. Eat with them and pray with them. Be prepared; a prediction according to the scriptures is that not everybody gets it and not everybody will understand, and we need to be at peace with that knowledge.

This week. Go home, interact with your neighbor and invest in your broken relationships. Pursue a relationship with those who think differently than you.

Know that humans love pursuing the truth because by doing so, we never have to struggle with the truth that we find. Dwell on the idea that our world likes to pursue the truth, yet we do not recognize truth when we see it. Enjoy the moments of truth, and give thanks for the instances of clarity.

Fight your natural urges and your desire for absolute truth. As a human, that is a joy that we will only see in the presence of God when we are allowed to enter in the Glory of God.

Consider what is more important: pursuing the truth or accepting the truth that by grace God has put in your heart. Do

...welling in the truth be wedged by the desire to attain more truth. Amen.

Remembering Your Baptism

What is the earliest and most painful experience that you can remember? For me, it was riding shotgun with my dad, on his Ford Fargo, and then having his metal radio—that was unplugged—gashing my right leg, I still that scar.

What is the earliest and most joyful experience that you remember? Playing with my great Uncle Dimas, and waiting for him to cut a Mutant Ninja Turtle Mask out of a pair of pants that he was making for a customer. He was a local seamstress.

What is the earliest time that you felt lost, yet safe that you remember? The time that I was on Uncle David's back swimming towards an open ocean's buoy.

You might say. That's an odd way to start your sermon, but I would say that those feelings of pain, joy, loss and safety come together like a rushing river for those of us that were baptized today.

You might say, "What?" And I will say, "Yes".

Painful; whether you knew it or not, you are calling Ainsley and Dante sinners (The infants that were baptized today). And they have done nothing really besides behaving like babies.

Joyful; whether you knew it or not, you are telling them not to panic, that their parents and the Church have promised them to teach them about our Christian faith and to walk with them in their victories and failures.

Church, we have celebrated a sacrament that proclaims that Ainsley and Dante were lost, but that now by faith, they are safe. What a day for these children of God! I wonder if they will remember their baptism. I wonder what they will remember about this day?

For many of us, remembering our Baptism is pretty difficult, especially if your parents believed in infant baptisms. But it shouldn't be difficult to remember.

The liturgy of baptism is the same and the best way to remember your baptism is to see someone experiencing the same thing. In essence, if you have seen one baptism you have seen them all. But this is not to say that baptism is not important, it is quite the opposite. Baptism is to a Christian as breathing is to a person that is alive.

Breathing happens every day, but it doesn't mean that breathing is less important. Baptisms happen every day, doesn't mean that Baptisms are less important. Just like breathing, we take our baptism for granted.

Just like we take for granted the prayer of Mary, and just like we take for granted the 4th Sunday of Advent because we are ready to have Christmas.

To take Christmas seriously, you need to know Mary's prayer. If not you are at the risk of seeing Christmas as a holiday created by corporate America rather that the time of anticipation and the birth of our Christ. Mary's prayer isn't just a prayer of thanks:

It is a prayer of announcement. It is a prayer of anticipation, and it is a prayer of acknowledgment.

Mary's prayer isn't just her prayer; it is a prayer that started even before her. If you pay attention to our reading of Micah, you will see that in there they were already talking about the birth of Jesus in Bethlehem.

Mary's prayer isn't a prayer that ended with her either; it is a prayer that we continue today in our Baptism. In Baptism, we continue the announcement of the salvific acts of Christ, we anticipate Jesus return, and we acknowledge the grace of our God.

In anticipation of the Birth of Christ, take some time to remember your baptism, but do not do it out of obligation because you acknowledge that Jesus was born and was killed because of you. Rather do it out of Joy! Let us remember with joy our own baptism.

Revisit the significance of it by praying through the baptismal liturgy; Reverend Lindsey's wonderful insert should help you with that. Look at yourself in the mirror and remember the words that were said.

If you are a parent, it's vitally important that you talk through this with your children. You are responsible for things like their health and wellbeing; you make a decision about surgeries and what foods they eat; then you are also responsible for them to grow knowing about our Lord Jesus.

Even if your child is 23 or 52, it should be your priority to help them remember with Joy their Baptism, knowing that the best way to remember their baptism is to witness and belong to a community of faith.

If you are a Christian and you are an adult, and your children are children, is your responsibility to bring them to church. Just like it is your responsibility to take them to the doctor when they are sick, or to make sure that they go to school even if they do not want to go. It is your responsibility to bring them to church for worship, fellowship, and mission. If you do not, you will be held responsible, not by the Church, but by Godself.

If you are a Christian and you are an adult, and your children are adults, your responsibility changes. You are not responsible for bringing them (that was the easy part). In this case, your responsibility is to encourage them constantly to go to church; you do it by leading by example and word. Just as you would do if they are sick or they do not have a job, and they need to get a job, you never quit. Now, if you are a child, youth, young adult, you are also responsible to bring your parent to church, or to encourage them to congregate.

And so, the list never ends. We could talk about the responsibility of one another, but the trick is about remembering with joy your own baptism.

There are not enough hours to talk about the levels of responsibility, but ultimately the very first step is to remember with joy your baptism.

May you remember that in baptism you are claimed. May you confess that you belong and that you play an important role in the announcement, in the anticipation and the acknowledgment of God, Amen.

Mario Version 20.1.4

This is the Mario version 20.1.4 loaded with lots of extras. This version of Mario might look the same around the edges, but nonetheless, he is an older version. At the time, it didn't have all the upgrades of software and hardware that the new version will have which is being released on January 1st

Mario was made in Colombia but quickly was brought to America for improvements and for many upgrades like ministry and worship capabilities and great an enhancement as the Melissa Staniec 20.09, now known as Mel Bolivar 20.14 which is an outstanding organism.

This version that you see here is also known as El Muñeco, (the Old Year Doll) which traditionally is burned in the streets of Colombia as a symbol of out with the old, in with the new.

He was in the midst of a busy schedule between his work at the law firm, pulpit supply within the Miami Valley Presbytery and his search for his first ordained position in a ministry setting.

One thing for sure was that he was itching to be in full-time ministry. The story goes a bit like this. Omar and Gina (the parents of the handsome Mario) had just arrived in town and were talking about life, work, and ministry. I don't remember if that was the first time or not, but Mel with almost a prophetic voice said to them, "Something is going to happen in April." And guess what church, on April 3rd we accepted the terms of call, and on April 27th we met you, and you accepted me as your new associate minister.

Around the same time just before my birthday, the door partners of the law firm invited me to take a more involved role within the firm that I used to work with. One of them knowing me very well asked me what my goals and objectives were for the year 2014, to which I replied to find a full-time ministry and receive my ordination within the PCUSA.

For a while now I have known what I wanted to do with my life, but more importantly, I knew what God was calling me to be. I guess I am that type of person. When I met Mel, I called my mom the very next day and told her that I had met the woman that I was going to marry, and about two days later I asked her, "Mel, do you want to me my girlfriend?" just like it was 8th grade.

It is strange; I guess I am the type of person that is encouraged by the awareness that, "You lose more in the indecision than by a bad decision."

I am the type of person that has a long-range projection. The "Let's go get the job done", the person that will "See things through." You put a goal in front of them, and that is all they need. Often the details are blurry and the goal is the only thing that is somewhat clear.

Now there is another type of person with a round range projection; the "Let us explore" person that does a bit of everything. They do not like just completing things. They like to explore all their abilities and talents.

And then there is a type of person with an immediate range projection; the "I am happy, I am content" people, the ones that look like they are comfortable with the living in the now.

Are you a long, round or immediate range projection kind of person? Do you find yourself having a little bit of everything, or maybe just two? Or maybe neither of them?

Well, let us rejoice that we are not all the same! God made you that way for the benefit of all and God's glory. Imagine what they the world would look like if we would all behave, think and act the same.

We are all creation of God, adopted by God, but we are not the same because it wasn't God's desire for us to be the same. It is only natural that we do not want the same things. Some people want better jobs, some people what to develop their talents and some people just want to survive, yet we are all created for the same purpose.

But how is that even possible? We are free to desire different things and are given distinctive talents to accomplish clashing goals, yet we are encouraged to have the same purpose?

It is quite simple. We read it in Psalm 148 this morning. "Praise the Lord; Praise the Lord" says the scriptures. We all have a place in the praising band, and we are called to praise God with what we have. It doesn't matter is you sing low of if you sing high.

That is our purpose, but you have the freedom to do it your way, just like all the supernatural beings, animals, monsters, elements and things that we read in the continuing verses. And just like that, the sky is the limit.

In roughly 85 hours (December 31st) you will be able to reset the bar; to make New Year's resolutions to yourself, your family, to your church and God.

The usual suspects are: to lose weight, volunteer to help others, quit smoking, get a better education, get a better job, save money, get fit, eat healthy food, manage stress, manage debt, take a trip, reduce, reuse, and recycle and drink less alcohol.

Church, for the next year I will challenge you to rethink New Year's Resolutions. Sure, you might think I am talking about a new toy like a smart watch to keep track of your progress or a new App, but my suggestion is more God and less you.

It is not to look for a quick fix, rather a meaningful change of outlook.

My top four reminders to a meaningful New Year's Resolution are:

1. With God, resolutions do not expire: People, family, the system, your job, your energy, and the market will fail you, but God will not fail you if you seek God's guidance. Through your community, study, worship and prayer you will find the encouragement to continue.

2. God is eternal, and God's promises are eternal: With God, the fullness of time, is a reality. We are a new creation, and through the salvific acts of Jesus Christ, our sins are forgotten. We are no longer slaves of the law; now we are children of the covenant, rightful owners of all blessings between heaven and earth

3. Gratefulness is the beginning: Don't limit your time of prayer. Prayer allows you to refocus your goals and your energy. Ask God to work in your heart, mind and your desires. The problem with our passions is that our eyes desire what our heart cannot handle. Often, we want and desire things because we want instant gratification and do not look at the long-term danger. Acknowledge that you want God to be in control and that you are a loyal member of God's house. Remember that you are part of the creation and find joy in praising God at all times but especially when you are blue or in despaired.

4. Be an agent of improvement: While in prayer, do not ask for ungodly things, and while in public always, behave as if your

friends from church were with you. Be a cheerful giver of money and time. Be attentive to where your money and time go, usually there you will find your heart. Be mindful and honest with strangers, and twice as much with those who you know well.

Encourage your little ones always to pray and to be grateful to those around them. Help those around you to improve in whatever way is possible

There is no Old versus New.

In Colombia, we make the "Muñeco" with old clothes as a symbol of the Old, and we are encouraged to make New Year Resolutions to forget the old, and start by reinventing yourself by burning the Old Muñeco.

With God and by God we can do just that but in a more real and effective way.

God knows our brokenness; God likes you the way you are. God does not want to destroy what makes you, you. Remember that you are not only God's creation, but you are God's child.

God wants to improve who you are. God will give you new clothes and a new identity without destroying your old essence.

Recognize that the resolutions with God do not expire, starting your day in prayer, always seeking to impact those around in a positive way, and knowing that God did not come to this world to destroy you or cause you harm will allow you to become successful in the new year.

Always be mindful and protective of your time with God, as God is often communicating with you. Know that no matter what you do in life and who you are, and what is your role in creation, there is always a place for you in the praising band.

God calls you by name, and more than anything God knows you by name. May we remember to keep and maintain our hopes within the knowledge of our Lord, who gave us freedom from our sin, and claim us as his family. Amen.

www.ingramcontent.com/pod-product-compliance
Lightning Source LLC
Chambersburg PA
CBHW072041110526
44592CB00012B/1517